Frankie San

Frankie San

A Burning and Shining Light for Christ

S. K. Wilkinson

We love hearing from our readers. Please contact us
at www.anekopress.com/questions-comments with
any questions, comments, or suggestions.

The author attempted to keep the details in this book accurate according
to the information we had at the time of writing. In order to maintain
anonymity, the names of some individuals and places have been changed.

Printed in the United States of America
Aneko Press
www.anekopress.com
Aneko Press, Life Sentence Publishing, and our logos are trademarks of
Life Sentence Publishing, Inc.
203 E. Birch Street
P.O. Box 652
Abbotsford, WI 54405
BIOGRAPHY & AUTOBIOGRAPHY / Religious
Paperback ISBN: 978-1-62245-647-5
eBook ISBN: 978-1-62245-648-2
10 9 8 7 6 5 4 3 2 1
Available where books are sold

Contents

Author's Apology vii

Prologue...ix

Ch. 1: Tokyo 1

Ch. 2: Landing in America...9

Ch. 3: Seminary Years...15

Ch. 4: First Years after Seminary...31

Ch. 5: "Peace of God" by Frankie San 37

Ch. 6: The Newsletter...41

Ch. 7: Teaching..49

Ch. 8: Raging Riots 59

Ch. 9: Refuge in a Library 65

Ch. 10: Christmases in Confinement 77

Ch. 11: Felons for Friends..91

Ch. 12: Triumph, Tragedy, and Sadness.....................................125

Ch. 13: Citizenship..137

Ch. 14: Beyond the Prison Walls...141

Ch. 15: Thoughts from Death Row..149

Ch. 16: Broad River Correctional Institution..............................155

Ch. 17: Life after CCI...159

Ch. 18: Retirement...169

Ch. 19: Passing the Torch...179

Ch. 20: Frankie's Wisdom 193

Appx. A: Biographical Sketch of Kyuzo Miyaishi 201

Appx. B: Frankie's Collections..203

Appx. C: Author's Last Words 221

Other Similar Titles...223

Author's Apology

Half a century. How do you write about fifty years of ministry? Fifty years of love and suffering? Yet Frankie San spent his life as a vessel of God's love, His vehicle to reach the unreachable, forgotten men.

One cannot understand such a life outside of the lives he served; the fifty years of his life are a tapestry of other lives woven together and named *Frankie San*. He gave his life for others, and all the men whose lives he touched became threads in this woven work of art.

The story of Frankie San could not be told without including some of the stories of the men behind the walls. Regrettably, I could not tell all, and I have chosen to use only first names for privacy's sake. These men are individuals – all different, yet all similar. The men's stories included in this book are only a portion of the many Frankie San's life touched, and while I wish I could have included all, I echo what the apostle John wrote of Jesus, *these have been written so that you may believe that Jesus is the Christ, the Son of God; and that believing you may have life in His name* (John 20:31).

- S. K. Wilkinson

Prologue

Well after midnight, Kyuzo Miyaishi, known to all as Frankie San, approached the last electrically operated gate as he exited the state penitentiary. The guard pushed the button, and the sergeant on duty laughed and said, "Frankie, where in the world did you come from? We had forgotten you were inside the walls. Did you have a nice party with the inmates?"

"Yes," Frankie replied in his thick Japanese accent, "I surery did, and I wish to stay awe night." Inwardly he thought how wonderful it would be if all these men could go home on this night, especially the younger ones who were away from home on Christmas Eve for the first time.

The desk sergeant said, "Well, Frankie, how does it feel to play Santa Claus?"

"They had nice time – eat turkey, open presents I bring, but now I feel like Cinderella when her party was over."

"Don't be sad, Frankie," said the sergeant. "You've done your best."

"Well, good night and Merry Christmas to you awe." Frankie San walked outside into the night. A few steps away, he stopped and looked back. One by one the lights flickered off all over the penitentiary as they always did, as if to coldly ignore the fact that it was Christmas Eve. He took a deep breath and looked up into the dark sky. The stars twinkled and seemed to sing with joy.

All over the world, people celebrated and went to parties, but Frankie had just spent Christmas Eve in a ward with fifty prisoners. Few people would believe the joy they shared together at their party behind the walls. He chuckled to himself as he recalled Mike, Bill, Joe, and Charles teasing him.

"Bingo, Frankie," they had bantered. "How about staying all night with us? We have an empty bed, and we won't charge you anything." Everyone laughed.

"No, I can't do that fellows. My mother told me not to associate with bad guys like you, and I must listen to my mother, you know."

"Good grief, Frankie. Don't you know we are really the good guys? We are all innocent; just ask us if you don't believe so," they snickered. "Frankie, we know you are a good guy too – when you are asleep." More laughter.

"Hey Doodle Bug," one of the men had called out. "Do you believe Frankie is really Santa Claus?"

"No, man. Santa Claus can't be that ugly." They all burst out in laughter.

A new inmate had approached Frankie and looked somewhat puzzled. He asked, "How much time have you got to serve?"

Frankie answered, "Oh, just life; that's all. That's not too much, is it?"

"No," he had replied nervously, "not if you say so, I guess." The whole ward erupted in shrieks of delight.

Frankie turned and walked toward his quarters. Many thoughts filled his mind as he lay down on his bed; he wondered why he chose to spend Christmas Eve as he did – away from society, among the outcast, in a lonely, ugly place. He gazed through the window at the sky and suddenly noticed a star brighten and then disappear. Then he remembered where

Jesus was born – in a lowly stable in Bethlehem nearly two thousand years ago. The Son of God and Savior of the world was not born in a beautiful place, and only a few people knew the real beauty in that manger.

Many are quick to notice the unpleasant things when they look with their eyes, but real beauty is seen and witnessed by a man's soul. In Bethlehem or in prison, there is ugliness, but just as the wise men found beauty in that city, so Frankie found beauty in that prison. Separated from the gaiety of society by prison walls, he experienced the true meaning of God's love by sharing the loneliness of a penitentiary Christmas with those who had no one to bring them happiness at this joyous time.

In the silence of his room, he whispered, "Happy Birthday, Lord Jesus." Then he went to sleep, knowing that only the stars and God could understand the peace and joy he felt.[1]

This is the story of one Frankie San, formerly Kyuzo Miyaishi, who left his homeland of Japan after World War II to serve his Lord in the prison system of South Carolina. In his unselfish manner, he walked with humility among the outcasts and shared the love of Christ with them. He presented himself as a living sermon – a sermon in shoes.

---

1   Adapted from "Once Upon a Christmas Eve," by Frankie San, in *Cell 55*, 1967.

Chapter 1

Tokyo

In September 1929, America was on the brink of the stock market crash that plummeted the world into the Great Depression. Japan struggled with little economic growth and its own financial instability. In addition to recovering from World War I, a massive earthquake had hit Tokyo in 1923 and killed more than a hundred thousand people. Suffering swept over the island even before World War II began, but a man was born during this time who would become a burning and shining light for Christ.

Kyuzo Miyaishi was born in the midst of that troubled time in Tokyo, Japan, to a Buddhist family where he already had a sister and two brothers. His father ran a small rice dealership, so rice was the main item of their diet. His mother cleaned the rice, and after school his older brothers, who were only fourth and sixth graders, took their bicycles and delivered fifty-pound rice bags to the neighbors. They were poor but didn't go hungry.

One day when Kyuzo was in second grade, he felt ill; his head hurt and his legs turned wobbly. He tried to walk, but the room went black, and he passed out. By the time the ambulance arrived, he was alert enough to realize what was happening, and he was scared to death. The emergency workers lifted him into the ambulance, and they took off down the street. Sirens blared and this little boy was petrified.

The doctors diagnosed him with a contagious disease (likely yellow fever), so he had to stay in the hospital without any visits from his family. No friends, no family, just long hours all alone. During those days, he tasted the loneliness that comes from being cut off from the world – a memory that would return to him years later.

When Kyuzo went back to school, he was behind in his lessons, which made him feel more alienated. He could not read as well as his classmates, and he strained over his math. He hated going to school when he felt so inadequate, but he went anyway.

Every morning eight hundred children gathered in the schoolyard, and the principal made a few announcements. Then they all turned toward the emperor's palace and bowed deeply. According to ancient chronicles, the gods created the islands of Japan and separated them from the rest of the world. Emperor Hirohito himself was considered a divine descendant of the sun goddess. He was the holy one, and the people gave him their lives regardless of the situation.

When Japanese children were born, the parents took them to the Shinto shrine to thank their god. When they died, their bodies were taken to the Buddhist temple for burial. Whenever they visited the Shinto shrine or the Buddhist temple, they washed their hands and rinsed their mouths with running water for purification before entering, even though they did not have a concept of sin.

Kyuzo prayed silently for the emperor to make him a smart boy, but Kyuzo never believed that prayer was answered. He struggled in school and felt like the dumbest pupil in the class.

One day Kyuzo heard a man on the street who beat a drum

and shouted, "Just believe Kirisuto Lesu (Christ Jesus), and you'll be saved. Come to our Sunday service."

He fascinated Kyuzo, but the children watched the man from a distance and whispered to each other, "They worship foreign god, Jew! We worship emperor, god!" A few of the intelligentsia, however, attended the church service. Even before the war, the Christian message was present on the streets of Tokyo.

When he was ten years old, Kyuzo rushed home from school and called to his mother, "Mama, Mama, the teacher said, 'Remember Pearl Harbor!' The war broke out today. Mama, where is Pearl Harbor?"

When World War II started, Kyuzo didn't even understand why they were fighting, but everyone was feverishly patriotic. Nationalist right groups had grown during the 1920s and 30s. Kyuzo loved his country, and with the young and old he was ready to die for the emperor and their "holy land." The next year Kyuzo's oldest brother died from tuberculosis, and his other brothers joined the navy as kamikaze pilots. As the war dragged on, B-29s flew overhead and dropped bombs all over the city, destroying buildings and houses.

As soon as Kyuzo finished eighth grade, he joined the Imperial Navy. He was fourteen years old and ready to die for his emperor. He thought dying in battle was honorable; he would be immortalized as a wind-spirit god. If he died for the emperor, his soul would go to a special shrine, Yasukuni Jinja, in Tokyo, and he'd become a war deity – or so he thought. Because they expected an invasion, Kyuzo volunteered to carry a land mine into an enemy tank, a dry version of the kamikaze pilot, committing suicide for the sake of the emperor he worshipped. Fifteen months later, however, two atomic bombs dropped on Hiroshima and Nagasaki. Emperor Hirohito made the declaration that they had to stop fighting, and he even confessed that he was not a god after all.

That surrender was hard to believe because it swept away more than twenty-six hundred years of Japanese history, but realizing that the emperor was not god was even more difficult. He was just a man. How could that be? How could the Japanese people and soldiers carry on? They had been ready to die for the emperor, but now they were defeated. They were so ashamed, but somehow they had to keep going.

Kyuzo and his brother went back to a ruined Tokyo. Most of the city had been destroyed. His father ran a small restaurant during the war instead of the rice store, but his mother had escaped to the countryside with the other children. Food was scarce and all of it was rationed. Every month each person received a ration book, but they ate anything that was considered edible.

Black markets were wide open, and black-market food was necessary to survive. One judge refused to eat any black-market food, just out of principle. Because he only ate rationed food, he starved to death. Rice was in short supply, and Kyuzo's family became desperate.

Kyuzo's father joined several others who went to Okinawa to bring back sugar, but when they returned to the harbor, an inspector became curious about the boat and wanted to check its cargo. All of the others fled, but Kyuzo's father remained with the boat. He took all of the blame. Kyuzo said, "My father had strong guts." His brother sold Kyuzo's overcoat, even without asking him, so he could hire a lawyer for their father, but he still had to serve three months of the one-year sentence in prison.

A few years later after the family was reunited, Kyuzo's parents were having problems. Not only the country, but also the family fell apart. Kyuzo's life was falling apart too. His discouragement turned to depression. His mother took the children and settled in a different house a few blocks from his father's restaurant, and Kyuzo and his older brother had to support the family.

He wanted a new life, so he found a job at an American soldier's house. He became the family's houseboy as he cleaned the house, washed the dishes, and took care of the babies. He worked hard and supported his mother and siblings.

When Kyuzo turned twenty-three, he decided to go to high school at night, so he quit his job. He found another job where he could work in the daytime and attend school in the evening. He thought he could find what he was looking for in education, but his effort was in vain. Life was still meaningless; his depression turned to despair. One night he went to a drugstore and bought sleeping pills. As he walked home, his legs wobbled like that long-ago day when he fell ill at school. Somehow he managed to put one foot in front of the other until he reached home. With a deep breath and trembling, sweaty hands, he struggled to open the bottle. Finally, he won the battle with that bottle and gulped down ten pills. He thought his misery would end that night, but late the next day he woke up. He was defeated; he couldn't even die. Tired and miserable, he believed no one understood his problem.

Four years later Kyuzo still floundered, but he had an opportunity to go to Hosei University. He was the first one in his family to get a university education, but he still didn't know what he was looking for. One evening as he waited for a train on the station platform, he suddenly heard a beautiful melody that he recognized from years ago: "Softly and tenderly Jesus is calling." The song touched his heart.

During his third year of university, he headed home one night, and on the corner he saw a man who was giving out little Bibles. The man held one out to Kyuzo – a Bible from the Gideon Society. Kyuzo took it and started reading it that night.

Later he also met an American missionary who had a

Bible class in his home. He told Kyuzo that Jesus said, *Follow Me, and I will make you fishers of men* (Matthew 4:19). Kyuzo attended the class, and for the first time he heard the gospel of God's forgiving love in Jesus Christ. He was awed by the God who willingly died for the sake of His people instead of people dying for their god.

Kyuzo read about a man called Jesus. Who was He anyway? A year later as he read one night, he heard a strange voice:

> *Peace I leave with you; My peace I give to you;*
> *not as the world gives do I give to you. Do not let*
> *not your heart be troubled, nor let it be fearful.*
> (John 14:27)

The words of the Bible came alive, and Jesus spoke to him; He brought Kyuzo His peace. Suddenly his hopelessness turned into great expectation for this new creation, and he responded, "Yes, Lord Jesus Christ, I will transfer all my faith to You and follow wherever You lead." Kyuzo turned from his belief in Buddhism to a totally committed, single-minded devotion to Jesus. His spiritual wall had crumbled.

Soon after this, a young missionary heard his story and approached him. He invited Kyuzo Miyaishi to Columbia, South Carolina, to attend Bible college. By the time Kyuzo was ready to graduate from Hosei University, the missionary had arranged for him to come to America to study the Bible.

The day Kyuzo went to buy his one-way ticket to America at an agency, he saw an elderly American lady who was attempting to communicate with the Japanese ticket agent. That agent didn't quite understand what she wanted, but Kyuzo did. He told the ticket agent, "She want privacy. She want two tickets for privacy. She stay in double room – alone."

When they left the ticket office, he became her personal

guide, and they went sightseeing together. He showed her parts of Tokyo that she never would have seen otherwise, and he gave her insight into Japanese character and customs.

The day came, however, for Kyuzo to leave. He boarded the ship while his parents, four brothers, two sisters, a nephew, nieces, and friends stood looking out over Yokohama Harbor. "Look over there! He is waving to us! See!" his sister exclaimed.

"He won't come back anymore, will he?" Etuko whispered to her brother Kazu.

"That is right, he says he must go. The Man has called him," he replied.

Gentle tears gave way to sobbing as they watched the great ship disappear over the horizon. On deck, Kyuzo watched his family until the ship had pushed off toward the sea. That was it. No turning back. He had two suitcases, a Greyhound bus ticket from San Francisco to Columbia, South Carolina, and a hundred-dollar check. No guarantee of the Bible school scholarship or anything else. He remembered that Jesus had said, *He who loves father or mother more than Me is not worthy of Me* (Matthew 10:37).

With Kyuzo gone, Etuko guided and chauffeured the American lady around the city, but none of them knew why he had met her at this time. The Lord seemed to be arranging his future even through this stranger.[2]

---

2   Adapted from "Man from Tokyo," by Frankie San.

Chapter 2

Landing in America

In 1961 Kyuzo Miyaishi experienced what the Pilgrims must have experienced when they landed at Plymouth Rock. He too arrived in this land with little or nothing except the vision that the divine hand of God seemed to be molding America. The nation was enthralled with the young president, John F. Kennedy. He was a president who promised to send men to the moon and establish a Peace Corps to serve the poor around the world. Proud Americans shared his willingness to build a foundation for world peace. The enthusiasm of the young people for their country was explosive and contagious to a young Japanese man struggling for a new identity. It was exciting! It was the very best of times! This nation and Kyuzo Miyaishi were on top of the world!

As the American President Line approached San Francisco Bay early one morning in June 1961, several hundred people on deck became very quiet and stared at the little island (Alcatraz) a short distance away. Chu, a young Chinese student, whispered with broken English, "Very bad guys are locked up on that island behind those walls – Al Capone, Machine Gun Kelly, Baby Face Nelson! They are bad, bad news!"

A few of the young people beside him nodded silently and gazed at the island in the foggy bay. A few thousand on board were young Chinese, Korean, Filipino, and Japanese students who left Yokohama Harbor two weeks earlier. They left their native countries and sought new adventures in this great nation, the land of opportunity.

To many Americans they were quarter-moon-eyed foreigners – all with black hair and all looking alike. Kyuzo was one of them who sought his unknown future, believing and following the Master's footsteps. If they had arrived in New York Harbor, the Statue of Liberty would have welcomed them; but instead, Alcatraz Island welcomed them – a prison for the worst of the castaways. That fact gave Kyuzo a strange feeling. Imprisoned men, alone on an island.

As the ship passed under the Golden Gate Bridge, the travelers gathered their belongings, bade farewell to each other, and departed in different directions. Most of their destinations were in the state of California, and most didn't even know where South Carolina was.

Kyuzo took a taxicab and headed to the Greyhound bus station. Before he headed to South Carolina, he wanted to visit the home of the missionary he had met in Tokyo. He walked up to the ticket counter and politely said, "One Tulock ticket please."

The ticket agent replied, "What's that, young man? Tulock? I've got no Tulock ticket. Where is that place anyway?"

"What you mean you got no ticket for Tulock?" Kyuzo thought all Americans were very kind, but now, here he was the foreigner trying to communicate. Kyuzo was irritated.

"Let me see, young man! Write it down on this paper."

"Here, T-U-R-L-O-C-K!"

"Oh, Turlock, California!"

"That's what I said!"

"Never mind, here's the ticket." He handed the ticket to Kyuzo and smiled.

That was the first of Kyuzo's awkward moments of communication. He thought his English was quite good, but in the Japanese language, there is no sound for *l*, *r*, or *th*. They cannot pronounce or hear those sounds correctly but instead say, "Sank you," for "Thank you."

In spite of this difficult beginning with the English language, in just a few years this young Japanese man would teach illiterate prisoners southern English in the Deep South.

That first summer in America, though, proved to be a difficult time for Kyuzo. He stayed with the missionary because his government had only allowed him to take one hundred dollars with him, and he needed more money. A Japanese man managed a peach orchard nearby and hired Kyuzo to pick peaches for seventy-five cents an hour. Each peach had to be a certain size or it was discarded on the ground to rot. Frankie had been so poor in war-torn Japan that such wasteful excess seemed unreal to him. Was this such a bountiful nation that it could throw food away? Nevertheless, he picked and saved and picked and saved. By the end of the summer, he had saved two hundred dollars, which is what he needed to get to South Carolina.

Once he arrived at Columbia Bible College, money was not his only difficulty. With such limited English skills, communication continued to be an issue. The school was small – only about a thousand students, and they were all younger than Kyuzo. The multitude of rules was like a noose around his neck. He did not understand them, and he thought they were too strict.

Frankie's dream of life in America turned into a nightmare. Although he had taught English to Japanese children while at Hosei University, he could not understand the language Americans spoke. He could not follow the lectures or complete his lessons. He had no money and was too proud to ask for help.

Frankie wanted to go home, but he felt too much like a failure. Once again, he thought of suicide.

However, the friendship that Kyuzo had developed with the American lady in Tokyo had greater implications than he had realized, and it all worked together for his well-being at this time. She knew he was attending Columbia Bible College in South Carolina, which was the alma mater of the missionary who had led him to Christ. As it happened, her son, Don, and daughter-in-law, Ellen, lived in a small town about thirty miles from the school. Her son was a judge advocate at Shaw Air Force Base. This lady wrote to her son about Kyuzo, who was now known as Frankie San, and urged him to visit Frankie.

Don called the college and was able to arrange to meet Frankie for dinner. When they arrived and asked for Frankie, one of the students said, "Oh, you mean 'the Jesuit.'"

Don thought this was strange until he caught a glimpse of their new friend in his dark kimono. The sight of this Japanese male wearing a kimono seemed to make the term *Jesuit* appropriate.

They dined at the Officers' Club at Fort Jackson in Columbia, and Frankie was very pleasant but withdrawn. Several servicemen who were at the club that night had been stationed in Japan, so they came over to the table, introduced themselves to Frankie, and talked about Tokyo. Then he brightened up. He was obviously very homesick, but something else also seemed to bother him.

On the way back to the college, Frankie San, in a very small voice, asked if either of them smoked cigarettes or drank alcoholic beverages. At that time Don did smoke, and both of them occasionally had a martini, so they were honest and told him so. Frankie began to weep bitterly. Evidently, the faculty and students at the college told him that drinking and smoking were sinful, and no good Christian associated with people who committed those kinds of sin. Furthermore, they had told this young Japanese man, who had been raised in a culture where men and women bathed together in public bathhouses, that mixed swimming at a public beach was also a sin. When Frankie had shown them a postcard of the beautiful stained-glass window in the Washington Cathedral depicting a modernized view of the ascension, the faculty was shocked. But for Frankie San, the culture shock was proving to be too much to cope with.

Don and Ellen invited Frankie to spend the Christmas holidays with them in their home. He accepted even though he was quite withdrawn the first week. During the second week, he relaxed, and at a gala celebration at Shaw Air Force Base on New Year's Eve, he may have been the only completely sober person, but he danced more and harder than anyone and had a better time. Don and Ellen had never seen the "Jesuit" happier, which convinced them that they had to find another school for their new friend.

They called a friend, Chaplain Virgil Schulein, a Lutheran minister, who attended classes at the Lutheran Theological Southern Seminary in Columbia. Don talked to Virgil about Frankie San, and they arranged a meeting with Dr. Reinartz. Frankie thought he was going to have dinner with Don's military friends, but he met the president of the Lutheran Theological Southern Seminary instead. Dr. Reinartz was intrigued with Frankie, as were the other faculty members who were present. Though his English left a lot to be desired, Dr. Reinartz became his new sponsor and accepted him as a provisional student at the Lutheran Theological Southern Seminary.[3] He was like a frightened, lost dog in bad shape.

In the end, Frankie's kindness to the elderly American lady in Tokyo led him to the connections he needed to enter the seminary. Was it a chance happening? Or was God directing his paths?

---

3   Adapted from "A Happening," by Don Hon.

Chapter 3

Seminary Years

Roommates

Dr. Reinartz worried about this sad-looking Japanese student, so he took him under his spiritual wing and became Frankie's guardian. Poor Frankie; he could hardly read the Bible or speak English. Sometimes Dr. Reinartz called Frankie into his office. Frankie always feared that he'd say, "Frankie, you should go back to Tokyo," so he hung his head in sorrow and shame.

Instead, Dr. Reinartz always smiled and said, "Frankie, how are your studies coming along? Do your best and don't worry too much. How are your finances? Do you have enough clothes? Don't worry about what people say. Your study is important and visiting the jails is important. Do what you believe and follow Christ; He'll guide your way. Here, Frankie, someone has sent me this gift for you." He encouraged Frankie and helped the other professors and students pay special attention to the student from the Orient.

One day Dr. Reinartz sent word to a student, Peter Setzer, that he wanted to see him in his office. Poor Peter wondered what kind of trouble he was in, so he felt temporary relief when Dr. Reinartz said, "Peter, we need your help. We have accepted a new student, a young Japanese man, a recent convert from Buddhism to Christianity. We want you to be his mentor and roommate. He doesn't speak fluent English, and he is weak in many of the academic requirements for admission to the seminary, but we feel led to suspend some of the requirements in his case."

Dr. Reinartz had the grace and wisdom to recognize a diamond in the rough, a rare soul who had the potential to make an immense impact on the seminary community and perhaps the world at large. It was a tough call for the president, but when the Lord lands a special orphan baby on your doorstep, you make room in the home.

So, Frankie and Peter became roommates. Never had two more unlike characters survived under the same roof. Peter had just roared in from the American range, calloused from breaking horses and calloused around the heart from living a head-'em-up, move-'em-out approach to people and an I'll-yank-it-out-by-the-roots approach to problems. Frankie, on the other hand, only came up to Peter's rodeo belt buckle. He was everything Peter was not – humble, sacrificial, soft-spoken, quick to cry, and non-combative.

They shared a common faith, a common room, and a common desire to graduate, but that was all. Peter hung up his guns, spurs, and whip on one side of the room; Frankie hung his bamboo Buddhas, silk tapestries, and hakata dolls on the other – two worlds called into unity by a common Christ.

At first, the change in schools seemed to have done little to help Frankie. He went for days without eating; once he stayed in bed for four days, sick with fright, disappointment, and shame. Peter tried to cheer him up, but with little success. With Peter's tutoring, though, Frankie's studies started going better.

In return for Peter's help with his studies, Frankie insisted on washing all of his clothes – by hand. Or, more accurately, by feet. Peter tried to explain that he was a proud, independent guy and could take care of himself, but Frankie became stern and said, "If I can no wash your clothes, I can no be your roommate!"

In the end, Frankie piled all of Peter's dirty clothes in a washtub, lugged it into the shower, dumped in soap and water, and stepped into the tub. He'd tread on those clothes for twenty or thirty minutes as though he were stomping on grapes for wine. Frankie smashed and splashed until Peter had the cleanest clothes at the seminary, and Frankie the cleanest feet.

Frankie's loyal servanthood embarrassed Peter on campus because Frankie would walk three paces behind him wherever they went. Peter was the master-teacher to Frankie, but Peter felt more like a mama duck. Finally he said, "Frankie, would you stop following me and come up beside me?" Peter detected amused bystanders who noted the way Frankie always seemed to be running to catch up – Peter and his shadow. However, when Peter stopped walking, so did Frankie.

Some of the Japanese customs were strange for Peter – like when care packages came from Japan, and Frankie gave Peter a doll. Dolls and tough guys did not mix in Peter's mind, but he kept it (Peter later displayed it in glass in his living room). The Japanese junk food was another trial for Peter. One day he exclaimed, "This is guaranteed to make a Texas buzzard sick to his stomach." Some of it was laced so strongly with garlic that the odor didn't leave the room for four or five hours after Peter made Frankie quit eating. One day Peter got brave and tasted a little round thing, which he promptly spit out. "Yuck! That tastes like a rotten apricot that's been soaked in salt water!"

"That's what it is," Frankie answered.

Even worse was the seaweed soup that Frankie mixed up in the room. He reached in with his chopsticks and grabbed a long, soggy strand. Peter exclaimed, "That looks like wet toilet paper!" Frankie never batted an eye as he indulged, and Peter gained a new respect for Frankie's mettle.

In spite of the trials of two very different cultures living together, the blessings were profound. Particularly prized and cherished was the prayer life they shared – a new dimension in devotions developed for them. Frankie prayed in a reverent whisper that evoked images of a God of fearsome majesty. Through tears, he often trembled when he prayed. Somehow, God was close enough to hear his whispers and bent a willing ear to the self-effacing little man who called Him "Fathah." Many of Frankie's petitions were desperate pleas for strength to endure the overwhelming academic challenges bombarding a man who was new to the faith, the language, and the culture. Always, there was an underlying trust that the God who had guided him halfway around the world would not fail him.

Frankie's prayers, in broken English, were so simple, so disarmingly childlike, so honest an outpouring of personal devotion that Peter often wept with him. His sophisticated western reserve was cast aside as he surrendered utterly and completely to the Master. Many Americans, reared on John Wayne movies, find it nearly impossible to understand, let alone imitate, the total submission of the oriental man.[4]

Servanthood

Frankie repeatedly referred to himself as the least of the seminary students. In his eyes he was unimportant, a burden to President Reinartz, the seminary faculty, and his roommate; but in reality, Frankie was forever looking for ways to lighten the load of others. He gave away hundreds of things he had ordered from Japan. He gave away money. He cooked; he cleaned; he gave professional rubdowns. With his cultural

---

4   Adapted from "Frankie's Seminary Years," by Peter Setzer.

handicaps and bruising academic load, he was busier than the rest of the students, but he still managed to find time to show God's love to others.

Frankie appeared vulnerable in those days – as breakable as one of his delicate hakata dolls. Peter often tried to shield him from many circumstances, but that upset Frankie. As time passed, he came from behind the shield and threw himself into frightening tasks with reckless and faithful abandon. One time, though, Frankie did not return to his room until eight in the morning. He staggered in, bleary-eyed and smelling of cigar smoke and sour wine.

"Frankie, where have you been?" Peter asked him.

He explained, "I been downtown Columbia at storefront mission that reach out to derelicts. They have soup kitchen, little chapel, and bedroom where luckless person can spend night. I go to meet forsaken ones and assure that God love them."

Frankie was like a Daniel in the lion's den. He told Peter, "I climb up into top bunk and go to sleep. In bunk below was ex-convict, vicious killer. He creep up and raise his knife to stab me. I scream and sit up in bed so fast I smash head on low ceiling. I look down and see killer in his bunk; he snore away. I say, 'Must have been nightmare.'

"After hour or two, I sleep again, but murderer from below rise up again. I wake suddenly and bang head again; it bring me to reality." The night was a tough one for the meek, little Japanese man, but on that night he may have conquered his fear of convicts.

And not only may Frankie have conquered his fear, but he also determined to do something for these men. He found it hard to justify living in luxury on the spacious campus and eat gourmet meals without sharing with those less fortunate. He knew God loved them too, so he talked with the other students about having them over for a meal. The other students carefully explained why that simply couldn't be done, but to Frankie, that didn't seem right. He wanted to demonstrate love to these people.

Another student, Mark, often gave Frankie a ride home from the mission, so Frankie told him about his desire to have a special Thanksgiving dinner for these ex-cons and hoboes. "Where would you get the money for such a feast?" Mark asked.

"Well, all I have is enough for three dollars a person and for that I think we could get a nice meal."

"That's beside the point. These hoboes don't have any clothes to wear to a restaurant. You know what they wear; you know the condition of their clothes," continued Mark.

"I don't care what they wear! All I want is for them to have Thanksgiving dinner!" Frankie expressed his disappointment. He knew they only had ragged clothes. The rest of the way back to the seminary, he didn't talk to Mark. When they arrived, he jumped out and slammed the door. He ran into the dormitory, crawled into bed, and covered himself up – even his head. He was so angry he cried to the Lord, "All I want is to feed these men."

Early the next morning Mark poked his head into the room. "Are you there, Frankie? I went to see Dr. Reinartz this morning. He said it's okay to have a Thanksgiving dinner. You can have the dinner at our campus mess hall. What do you say to that?"

"Oh, thank you, Mark. Thank you, Lord."

Peter had also learned that when Frankie was moved to assert himself for Christ, all of his swashbuckling bravado was puny stuff compared to the Spirit working in Frankie. When Frankie was moved, Peter stepped back and followed. "Okay, Frankie, whatever you say, let's do it!"

They made the arrangements. Frankie wanted to have the whole motley crew over for the grand formal dinner of steak and shrimp instead of turkey. He planned to pay the bill and asked Dr. Reinartz to give a sermon. Eventually the idea caught hold among the students, and they provided the transportation and companionship.

The guests tried to wear their best clothes, but they had wrinkled shirts and old ties. Most had taken baths, combed their hair, and put on ties. Some came straight from work, so their clothes were sweat-stained and greasy. Some had scars on their faces and large, ugly tattoos on their arms. Each student took one guest and sat at a table. The headwaiter came around and took their orders.

Some men didn't have any teeth and had a hard time chewing their steaks; others picked the T-bones up with their hands and chewed the meat off the bone. One man tried to use his knife and fork so hard that a piece of steak fell to the floor. He just reached down, picked up the piece, and continued to eat as though nothing had happened.

An aged and broken ex-boxer stuffed his hat in his hands and looked worshipfully around the center. "I never have been to such a nice place as dis!" His had been a life too long serving as a human punching bag for prizefighters on their way up.

That night at the center, they were all treated like royalty, and they ate like royalty. When Dr. Reinartz finished preaching, the boxer brushed away tears, and maybe for the first time in years, he looked undefeated. He had won a prize after all!

Most students didn't know how to react to the guests' strange manners, but eventually they understood and enjoyed the meal. They had put on a great banquet; they had gone to the highways and hedges and compelled the dregs of society to come in.

After Dr. Reinartz spoke, Frankie stood by the door and said goodbye to the guests. The last poor man approached; he was bearded and wrinkled. He tried to say something, but the words would not come out. A tear ran down his cheek as he stood and gazed at Frankie. Suddenly, he grabbed Frankie and hugged him. Frankie could smell the body odor and grease, but he hugged him back – as if hugging his own father. Then tears flowed down his cheeks too. Without words, the man walked out into the darkness.

No seminary student of that generation would ever preach on the parable of the great banquet without remembering that awesome, holy night when Frankie brought the derelicts to dinner. And, where did he get the money to buy all those steaks? Where did he get the money for anything? Only God knows. Frankie gave money away like Rockefeller – wherever he discovered pain and need.

Normally, Frankie was flat broke. When a book or tuition bill came, he'd say, "Don't worry, Peter, God will take care of me." A mysterious envelope would arrive in the morning mail with a check covering the amount due. If it was more than he needed, he gave it away before the week was over. He lived in near-poverty, but gobs of money passed through his hands. Peter concluded that God was his personal banker; money was like manna to be consumed before it soured.

One day Frankie spoke at a local church's vacation Bible school. He carted various oriental objects with him, which he incorporated into his witness for Jesus. Several days later he received a check for fifty dollars in the mail, an honorarium from the grateful congregation. When classes were over for the day, he hustled to town and bought fifty dollars' worth of candy, chewing gum, and little toys. He stuffed them in a big Santa Claus bag and returned to that vacation Bible school where he delighted the squealing children with a return for their generosity.

The next week more mysterious envelopes arrived. Frankie attracted blessings like a lightning rod. Was it because he would not possess them, but only distribute what God put into his trust? Peter envisioned Frankie, knee-deep in blessings, shoveling them out and away as fast as he could, and from another direction God shoveling into Frankie's pile as fast as He could. And God had the bigger shovel![5]

Teacher and Student

Frankie studied laboriously. He was not able to understand the lectures, so Peter reviewed his notes with him. Frankie rewrote simplified outlines, translated essential words he didn't understand, and filled the margins with Japanese jottings that were a mystery to Peter. Over and over that first year, Peter took complex Christian doctrines and reworded them in simplified terms until Frankie understood them. To Peter it was like the daily chore of putting fodder down so the little lambs could reach it.

Of course, this helped Peter also. The most surprising discovery was how accurately Frankie's personal faith reflected New Testament Christianity. Legalism, fanaticism, fundamentalism, and secularism had no place in Frankie.

One evening in the first quarter, Peter spent nearly two hours with Frankie. They reviewed class notes and the course book for an examination in their New Testament History class. Peter carefully explained the material, and Frankie gave silent nods of recognition as he politely jotted notes. With no way to tell how much Frankie comprehended, Peter paused for feedback. "Okay, Frankie, now you tell me. Tell me everything you know about Peter and Paul."

After a long silence, he said, "Peter and Paul? I don't know these men."

Peter couldn't believe his ears. He shot back, "You don't know Peter and Paul? Frankie, these are two of the most important people in the New Testament!"

Pained silence. His face flushed with oriental shame of the student who disappointed his teacher. He lowered his head to

---

5   Adapted from "Frankie's Seminary Years," by Peter Setzer.

hide the tears that betrayed the emotion. Then he confessed, "I don't know Peter. I don't know Paul. All I know is Jesus Christ. That's why I'm here at this seminary." Frankie was living 1 Corinthians 2:2 – *For I determined to know nothing among you except Jesus Christ, and Him crucified.*

Peter felt like crawling into a hole. All Frankie knew was Jesus Christ. This dynamic little Christian knew Him like few ever have.

> *That I may know Him and the power of His resurrection and the fellowship of His sufferings, being conformed to His death.* (Philippians 3:10)

Peter watched Frankie's amazing ministry take shape, and all along the driving force was that he could know Jesus Christ.

All of the hard work paid off, and a high point for Peter was the day Frankie received an *A* on a final exam. Whatever joy Frankie felt, however, was quickly drowned in oriental embarrassment when he learned Peter had only received a *B+*. To Frankie this was unacceptable and intolerable. He rushed off to Dr. Schott. "Please, Mr. Professor. There must be some mistake. I got *A*!"

"No, Frankie, there is no mistake. You did a fine job. You deserve an *A*."

"Please change it, sir, to *B*! How could I do better than my teacher?"

The good professor smiled but insisted that Frankie keep his *A*. Peter had plenty of *A*'s, but the one that Frankie got was the best one Peter ever earned.[6]

---

6   Adapted from "Frankie's Seminary Years," by Peter Setzer.

Disillusionment

Though Frankie was thrilled to be studying in the seminary, he struggled to understand the American way of life. He found the freedom to speak out and act out without fear to be a true culture shock. In 1963, Madalyn Murray O'Hair founded the American Atheists Center and sued the city of Baltimore, which resulted in a United States Supreme Court decision to outlaw the practice of prayer and religion in public places. Then the beloved President John F. Kennedy was assassinated, and in 1966 the *Time Magazine* cover asked, "Is God Dead?" thereby insinuating that He was. In 1968 Robert Kennedy and Martin Luther King Jr. were assassinated. In addition to these tragedies, the country moved into what seemed to be an unending war in Vietnam.

For Frankie, in just a few short years the exciting, energetic, moral, new land had become something else. People were frustrated with the government, young people marched and bombed buildings, and they had sit-ins and turned to drugs to hide their pain. Frankie watched the young men come home from war, broken physically and mentally with no one to accept them. He related to these men as he had experienced similar feelings when he returned to a broken Japan.

Frankie watched as the voices of the secularists rose boldly and the Judeo-Christian society that he had come to be a part of became weak – its voice, faith, and influence in this wonderful country could hardly be heard. A cultural revolution was taking place, and the moral fiber of the land he had come to love was being torn apart.

Marriages fell apart; mothers went to work; children came home to empty houses. Family values vanished, and drugs seemed to be everywhere. Crime spread and the prison population skyrocketed. Frankie said, "To me it was like holding the hand of someone I just fell in love with and watching her die."

Prison

During Frankie's first summer in South Carolina, he worked at Angelo's, a small, quick-order restaurant that was two blocks from campus. Since his parents had owned a family restaurant in Tokyo, Frankie felt right at home in the kitchen. Angelo, a high-strung, good-natured Greek, was pleased to feature another foreigner in his little diner. Frankie humored his new friend by wearing his ankle-length kimono. What a sight! A Japanese served up French fries in a Greek restaurant with all the grace of Tokyo's finest.

Frankie always took good care of his kimono, but one day at closing time, it was raining outside. He was on foot and without an umbrella, so Frankie stripped down to his underwear, rolled the kimono into a ball, and dashed down Main Street, taking his eight-inch strides. Peter met him at the top of the steps just as he entered the dormitory.

"Oh no, Frankie! Did you run from Angelo's like that?"

"Of course," he replied.

"Frankie, do you have any idea what Americans think when they see a grown man running down the street in his BVDs? They'll think this seminary is an institution for the insane!" Frankie had lots to learn about Americans and their way of life.

Angelo's provided a big window to this America, and Frankie peered out inquisitively whenever he could. He saw what looked like school buses that had been painted white with bars on the windows and loaded with men. That did not make sense to him, so he asked, "Angelo, who are those men?"

"They're jailbirds, part of a chain gang. They leave every

morning and return to the prison walls every afternoon," Angelo replied in his teasing manner.

"Jailbirds? I never heard of those kind of birds. What's a chain gang?"

Angelo explained and told him that those men were imprisoned at night at the penitentiary on Gist Street and then bussed to a new prison work site each morning. Around four o'clock in the afternoon, the men were loaded up and bussed back to prison.

Frankie saw them pass each day, same schedule, always on time. Mist covered his eyes when he saw them; they seemed to be pathetic creatures that were caged like birds. The next morning he watched for them, and when he saw the buses coming, he shuffled to the corner and bowed low as they passed and waved to them. On their return trip in the afternoon, he did the same. Frankie chose to honor them.

The angry-looking, muscle-bound, tattooed inmates were understandably surprised. "Hey, dig that cat with the dress on! Look at that Jap! What's he doing? Who's he bowing to? Who's he waving at? Us? Can't be." They all thought he was a little weird.

The next time the buses passed Angelo's, several inmates stood up in the aisle of the bus and peered out to see Frankie again, smiling and waving. After the three buses had passed, he bowed deeply from the waist and continued to bow as long as the men could see him. The third day they watched for him, and this became a daily occurrence. He would wave, bow, and shout greetings that the men could not hear. The men began to wave back and the drivers honked their horns.

When every passenger returned a reverent oriental bow, pandemonium broke out on the bus, but the waving/bowing ritual continued, and inmates who were boarding fought over who would get the seats on the Japanese side.

One summer evening Frankie held up a sign as the buses passed by. "Must go Washington," it said. "Be back September." The next afternoon, the corner by Angelo's was empty. To the delight of the prisoners, however, the daily ritual began again in the fall.

Frankie told Peter about his bus experiences and his plan to meet these men from the cage. Peter replied, "Are you crazy?"

Peter's question came from knowledge of the prison and Frankie's naivety. Tom O'Brien described the environment best:

> There is a river, the Congaree, that flows past the Central prison in Columbia. This is a beautiful setting where horses were quartered during the Civil War, and where a dismal complex of buildings – some dating back to 1867 – now warehoused men. Thousands of times he had heard the gurgle of the river swallow up the screams of tormented men, the sobs of real and sham repentance, the rare laughter, the violence of fights, the rattle of bloody murder, escapes, riots, executions, and the continuous mournful songs of the lonely and forgotten. The river hears men curse God and curse even those who pray to God for their fellow prisoners being laid to rest with no hope of eternal life, in an unmarked and soon-forgotten grave.[7]

But with Dr. Reinartz's assistance and connections, Frankie was able to meet Ellis MacDougall, director of the South Carolina Department of Corrections (SCDC), and get permission to visit these men. When Frankie entered the prison yard, a number of inmates said, "Isn't that the funny little guy from the street

---

7   Excerpt from *Cell 55*, Christmas 2001.

corner?" Then others joined them and finally asked, "Hey, aren't you the little guy who bows down to us?"

"Yes, sir," he replied as he demonstrated his most gracious bow.

"Yeah, you're him, all right. Will you write to me? Will you come to visit me?"

It was a glorious moment for Frankie. Here were men who desperately needed honor that he could give, love that he could show, and a gospel that he could share. He began corresponding with several on a weekly basis, staying up long hours into the night to reply to their many questions and complaints. Night after night Frankie wrote to these men and sobbed as his heart ached for the plight of each one. For the first time, some of the inmates saw a light in their darkness. Jesus became a real person to them, even though he had slanted eyes, yellow skin, and talked so strangely they had to strain to understand him. While the other students at the seminary studied about Paul, Frankie was busy *being* Paul. He put into practice the lessons he learned and conversations he had with Jesus. *To the extent that you did it to one of these brothers of Mine, even the least of them, you did it to Me* (Matthew 25:40).

Soon Frankie visited the prison on a regular basis. He stood before the cells, placed his foot on one of the lower bars of the door, and leaned forward with his arm on an upper bar as he touched and shook hands with the man on the other side. He always brought the same message: "Christ loves you. I love you. Christ doesn't care what crime you committed; He will forgive you if you let Him." He listened and shared, and his circle of friends grew. Tough-as-nails convicts who protected themselves with a permanent defensive snarl and hearts of reinforced barb-wire melted under the spirit of the strange little man who cared about them. Something about this Daniel's vulnerability and selfless trust in the goodness of God and the humanity of the lions took the snarl out and put a light in a dark, lonely den.[8]

Frankie met one particular inmate named Bob that year who thought he was perfectly satisfied with his godless outlook on life. He had no faith in people and no belief in God. He wasn't especially interested in Frankie, but he watched. He was familiar with a fickle, demanding love that was self-seeking, but he wondered about the source of Frankie's love.

Bob slowly understood what Frankie was doing for the inmates and why. He realized it was because Frankie believed in God and acted according to how Jesus expected His followers to act. Bob recognized that Frankie's love was greater than human love. He also noticed how happy Frankie was. But the turning point for Bob was when he saw two other inmates undergo a transformation in their lives and attitudes. The change was so obviously to their benefit that Bob developed an acute thirst for what Frankie had and taught.[9]

Through His printed Word, God revealed Himself to Bob. The scales fell from his eyes and his chains were broken. The Lord set him free – a free man in a cell. Bob wept and wept and thanked the Lord for making him new.

> *If anyone is in Christ, he is a new creature; the old*
> *things passed away; behold, new things have come.*
> (2 Corinthians 5:17)

---

8   Adapted from "Frankie's Seminary Years," by Peter Setzer.
9   Adapted from *Cell 55*, August 1966.

Chapter 4

First Years after Seminary

Lutheran Children's Home

In their senior year at the seminary, the students all chattered about their calls to serve fine congregations that teemed with friendly, gracious, and generous people. Frankie jarred them a little when he expressed his desire to be called to the prison, a draconian dungeon built the year after the Civil War, where he would work among desperate and dangerous convicts in a dark den of depravity and despair. These same inmates loved Frankie and presented him with a new shirt and tie as a graduation gift. They expressed their regrets that "prior commitments" prevented them from attending the commencement exercises but assured him that they were with him spiritually. Frankie declared that the tie and shirt were the best he had ever received.

Dr. Reinartz, however, had another idea. He arranged for Frankie to work at the Lutheran Children's Home in Salem, Virginia. So, Frankie said goodbye to his prison buddies.

"I do not know what God has for me to do. If He wills it, I will come back to penitentiary and stay with you, my brothers, inmates, always." With those words, Frankie bade them farewell on his final visit to the South Carolina Department of

Corrections before leaving for the Lutheran Children's Home. Bob and another inmate waved to him as he turned and walked toward the front gate to the outside. Sharing a feeling of intense sadness, they turned and entered the hallway that led back to their cells on the inside. They knew they might never again see this little man with a heart larger than the twenty-foot walls around them and a love stronger than the steel of the bars.

In fact, most of the inmates believed they would never see him again, and their last minutes together were solemn. They feared that Frankie's devotion to those who need love would perhaps bind him to the children of the Lutheran Home so tightly that he would never return to the prison. They were also aware that Frankie only had a temporary extension of eighteen months on his student visa. If immigration authorities denied him citizenship or a renewal, he'd have to return to Japan, not the prison. For the prisoners who knew Frankie, it was the bleakest of days.

In a short time, however, letters from Frankie came to inmates. Letters to keep his memory alive, but more than that, the essence of Frankie's devotion to his brothers became a permanent part of the attitudes around the cells. A little more kindness toward one another. Second thoughts before spouting off. Always wondering what Frankie would say or do. Then, Frankie wrote monthly newsletters, which they avidly read and dubbed the *Adventures of Frankie San*. They laughed and they cried over the stories, and then they prayed for his well-being and return.

Frankie was able to visit the penitentiary two times for short visits that year. His friends in the prison rejoiced to see him and regretted his leaving, but they became stronger in their determination to live up to his expectations.

Frankie loved the children at the home, but his heart and mind were back with the prisoners. Those castaways were his brothers, and they needed him too; they were his passion. Just like the abandoned peaches left to rot in the California orchard, the lowly men were plentiful in this great nation. Frankie knew *the harvest is plentiful, but the workers are few. Therefore beseech the Lord of the harvest to send out workers into His harvest* (Matthew 9:37-38).

After a year, Director MacDougall at the prison decided to begin a rehabilitation program for the inmates and asked Frankie if he'd come back to teach basic courses to the guys. So began Frankie's official ministry in the prison. No one would have expected this, but God has His own strange ways. Frankie was His man to show the "birds" true freedom.[10]

Back to Prison

When Frankie returned to prison, he came bearing gifts – five hundred towels, to be exact. His Christian friends had donated these for the inmates. The "funny little guy" was concerned for all aspects of the prisoners' welfare, and he continued to solicit items for these castaways.

Frankie requested to be admitted behind the bars and pressed the commissioner of prisons until he accepted Frankie's "voluntary life sentence." Every man in prison was dying to get out, but Frankie was dying to get in! Frankie understood this lesson from the apostle Paul when he said, *I, Paul, the prisoner of Christ Jesus for the sake of you Gentiles* (Ephesians 3:1). The prisoners were his Gentiles; Frankie San was their Paul.

The first weekend back was a busy one. He spent all day Saturday and Sunday visiting his old friends and meeting new ones who had arrived at the institution during the past year. He went to their living quarters to talk with them, but he had been up until two in the morning writing letters and was too

---

10   Adapted from "Frankie's Seminary Years," by Peter Setzer.

tired to talk anymore. So he took a short nap on the inmate's bed. Frankie even stood in line in the inmates' cafeteria and ate with them.

He joined one of the teams for volleyball; he shouted and screamed with joy every time his team scored and moaned in anguish when they missed a return. "Get the ball! Don't drop it! One and two and last one. Let's skunk them out! Ha, they drop ball again. Japanese team won!"

He attended both the Sunday morning worship service and the Sunday evening Christian Fellowship Club meeting where he passed out towels and washcloths. At the end of the weekend, Frankie exclaimed, "We have so much fun; I'm going to stay here forever!"

With the beginning of a new week, Frankie's official duty as teacher began. Bob had been teaching his fellow inmates as a volunteer, so he supported Frankie as he taught the basic courses. They worked together, side by side; like Paul and Silas they sang hymns of praise to God in their imprisonment. They rejoiced in the peace of God because they knew the Father was with them.

After the inmates finished their daily work, they came to "school" to study from four o'clock to seven o'clock, for many of them had never had the opportunity to learn to read or write. Now they were willing. Bob read to them from the Bible, and they listened to God's Word eagerly. He patiently instructed the slow learners:

"All right, Jeter. What is this word? Oh, come on, you know this word."

"Well, let's see; I knew that word."

"Yeah, you knew that. You know, something you put on your head."

"I remember that – *wig*?"

"Oh no, Jeter, this word is not *wig*."

"Oh? That ain't right? Something you put on your head, huh?"

"If you're giggling, you know this word."

"I ain't giggling. I forgot."

"H-A-T, *hat*, remember? How about this word? This is what Jesus said: 'I am the ____.'"

"*Road*?"

"No, Pop, this is not *road*. What is it?"

"Well, I'm getting sleepy."

"That's no excuse. That's right – *way*. Good for you, Pop!"

"All right, next; if you don't know this word, I'm going to kick you out of the classroom. No, no, no; not *Dod*."

"G-O-D, huh? *God*?"

"That's right, God! Even if you forget your name, don't forget this word!"

The joy of teaching and learning caused Bob and Frankie to burst out in laughter with hearts as light as a feather. These were Bob's students, and Frankie was amazed at what God had been doing in his life and his ability to help these men.

"Well, Frankie, I'll see you in the morning," Bob said as the guard unlocked the iron door and he disappeared down the hallway. Frankie walked toward his room in the guards' quarters but immediately left to help an ex-inmate, Ronnie, who had been released. Frankie would find supporters for him and some clothes. Ronnie was headed to a trade school, but he wanted to teach a Sunday school class too. Frankie consistently worked to help transition his brothers back into society.

At 1:00 a.m. Frankie looked out his window and across the baseball field at a building where Bob and his other brothers were probably asleep, dreaming of the fun they had playing volleyball. He watched the big moon shine peacefully over the prison yard. Another day had ended.[11]

---

11   Adapted from *Cell 55*, June 1966.

Chapter 5

"Peace of God" by Frankie San

Peace I leave with you; My peace I give to you;
not as the world gives do I give to you. Do not let
not your heart be troubled, nor let it be fearful.
– John 14:27

Peace of God

It was the year 1960.

    I was struggling – my meaningless life desperately
       in Tokyo.

My life was a living death.

    I had no hope, no joy, no peace in my heart.

One quiet night in October I read the Bible.

    Suddenly I heard the voice from heaven!

The Lord spoke to me peacefully first time.

    Peace I leave with you; My peace I give to you;
Not as the world gives do I give to you.

    Do not let not your heart be troubled,

Nor let it be fearful.

My blind eyes were opened.
    The angels of the Lord sang His joyful and peaceful
Praising songs all night,
    Then disappeared.

The following year I followed His call
    And came to this land of milk and honey,
His promised land.
    CALIFORNIA HERE I COME!

I rejoiced and thanked Him.
    But within two months I doubted His call.
As soon as I started studying, I was lost completely.
    I couldn't follow the lectures.
I couldn't adjust to American cultures:

Fast moving society,
    Free expressing society.
I screamed in the dark night,
    "Lord, Lord – where is Thy peace?

Lord, don't forsake me.
    I'm afraid! I'm ashamed of myself.
Show me Thy peace."
    I struggled and suffered,
I cried and moaned.

I murmured,
    "Why do I have to live shamefully?"
My heart was torn to pieces.
    I was ready to give up.

But David sang,
    Even though I walk through the valley

of the shadow of death,
I fear no evil,
For YOU are with me.
I trusted in my Lord.

My second summer at the Lutheran Seminary
I saw the prison buses on Main Street
Early one morning.
Was it just an accident I watched these buses?

What in the world has my life
To do with the prison buses?
What has His peace to do with the rough inmates?

Yet, my eyes and my soul were fixed
On these buses like a magnet.
A few months later
I started to visit the inmates.

In the high walls
I faced their suffering and their sorrow.
I saw their families weeping.
I watched their children crying.

Lord, why do I have to watch their suffering and
their weeping?
Why do I have to carry their burdens?
Did the Lord not know
I had enough problems of my own?

Yet His calling words kept coming back in my heart.
Peace I leave with you;
My peace I give to you.

After five years struggling
The Lord showed me His peace.

His peace is different from what the world offers;
  Completely different from what I thought.

Only through my struggling
  I have found His peace.
To the world, the penitentiary,
  He showed me His beautiful creation.

These sorrowful inmates,
  Ashamed inmates,
Outcasts of society.
  Yet the Lord gives me His peace
Through the forgotten inmates.

I have found His peace in the hearts of the inmates.
  Behind the high walls
The Lord has brought me His peace.

And I will sing with the prophet Isaiah:
  Thou wilt keep him in perfect peace,
Whose mind is stayed on thee:
  Because he trusteth in thee. (Isaiah 26:3 KJV)

I will write praises with Paul from the prison:
  For He is our peace,
Who hath made both one,
  And hath broken down the middle wall
Of partition between us. (Ephesians 2:14 KJV)

Praise Him, Worship Him, Prince of Peace.
  Amen[12]

---

12 "Peace of God," by Frankie San, *Cell 55*, September 1966.

Chapter 6

The Newsletter

The *Adventures of Frankie San* was originally *The Gospel According to Frankie San*, and many hoped it would always remain the same. It was a collection of updates, joyful news, poetry, personal thoughts, and anecdotes by Frankie and the prisoners. Through this newsletter, Frankie communicated the good news that *there is joy in the presence of the angels of God over one sinner who repents* (Luke 15:10).

The new title for the newsletter, *Cell 55*, was Frankie's choice – chosen with good reason. In one of the maximum security cellblocks of that institution, in cell 55, God broke the chains of sin from one unnamed sinner who had worn them almost proudly for twenty years. Frankie prayed that God would echo forth from that cell, so he renamed his newsletter *Cell 55*.

The newsletter allowed Frankie to preserve stories and situations that would have been lost in the vast catacombs of memories. He wrote about prisoners, their lives, and their families. By living in the prison, Frankie was available at any time for the inmates, but in such an old building, conditions were not good. "Life in the sardine can" was the description that most people used for the South Carolina Central Correctional

Institution (CCI). It was a hellhole serving as a warehouse for
the outcasts of society – crowded living quarters, lack of privacy,
and century-old walls. Standing in lines for meals, waiting for
mail, and hoping for visits were the norm.

Frankie's accommodations were overcrowded with a hot
plate, an overused refrigerator, a leaking ceiling, and crumbling
plaster. Sometimes Frankie used an umbrella as he worked in
his room to keep from getting drenched as rainwater leaked
in. One day in August 1966, the temperature got up to 108
degrees, and melting tar dripped from the ceiling. It was so
hot his weight dropped from 125 pounds to 115 pounds. Yet he
admitted that he had never enjoyed a summer so much in all
his life that he did not care that he had not been to the beach
or the mountains.

Frankie found the newsletter to be a means of sharing the
unusual and remarkable situations of his unique life. These
experiences often occurred from the language barrier, but sometimes from daily misunderstandings. Also, the prison was so
big that some of the people still didn't know Frankie – who he
was or where he came from. He wore a white shirt and pants;
some of the guards and inmates even thought he was another
inmate. He would hear things like:

"Do you get a chance to go out?"

"Did you know that Japanese man's father is a
millionaire?"

At the guards' quarters, he'd answer the telephone
and hear, "What did you say? What are you anyway? Guard or inmate?"

Sometimes Frankie used the newsletter to inform his supporters of what the inmates needed. He had begun a towel

distribution service while he was at the Children's Home, but there were many more needs, including simple things like soap and personal items. He was aware also of the needs of some of the families when their breadwinner was in prison. They received baby gifts for newborns and one time he purchased a small bike for a five-year-old son of an inmate. The needs were continual, but Frankie persevered to provide what he could.

Communication

In one newsletter, Frankie wrote of one night when he stopped at a filling station. A young lady approached him and said, "Can I get in your car? I'd like to go home with you. . . . What! Your home is a penitentiary? You big liar!" She slapped his face and disappeared.

More misunderstandings occurred when Frankie met with a policeman who yelled at him. "Young man! You are blocking the traffic!"

"I'm awfully sorry, officer. I did not mean to turn right from middle of street. I got confused, sir. I wanted to turn to left street, but it said, 'No Left Turn,' so I drove to next corner and again, 'No Left Turn.' Finally, I was confused at middle of street."

"Where are you from?"

"From Tokyo, Japan, sir."

"Where do you live?"

"In penitentiary."

"You live in the penitentiary? From Japan, studied at the seminary, and just got back from the Children's Home in Virginia? You confuse me! I'll let you go this time, but you stay in there!"

"Yes, sir! I'll stay there forever. Thank you, sir." Frankie was sweating and his heart was pounding as he maneuvered his car back to the prison.

Another incident that was preserved in the newsletter was

Frankie's first encounter with the Red Cross. One of the guys had said, "Frankie, don't tell me that you are coming with us!"

"Why not? I'll do anything you do."

"Oh, come on, Frankie. You don't need to give a pint of blood for twelve days of good time."

"I don't. But I give blood anyway – for the Red Cross."

As they gave their blood, Frankie realized that the inmates enjoyed the pretty nurses. Frankie's own communication with the nurses went something like this: "No sir, oops! Excuse me, I mean no ma'am. . . . Yes sir, oops again. I mean ma'am."

Frankie learned that the inmates gave one pint of blood to receive twelve days of good time off their sentences but also to watch the beautiful nurses at the same time. He reckoned they "killed two birds with one stone."

Later that same night he lay in his room and said, "I am sorry. I can't give you my blood tonight. I don't care how much emergency it is. I don't have any blood. You want to see my Red Cross card? You ask my roommate. He is young with lots of blood. Ouch, ouch! I'm going to kill you – you great American mosquito! Everything is so huge made in USA." There wasn't much sleep for Frankie that night as he battled the great American mosquito.

One day Frankie sat on Bob's bed, reading some letters from Virginia and dreaming of the Shenandoah Valley. Suddenly, he heard a scream. "Fraaankeeee!" Then someone threw something on top of his letters.

When Frankie saw it, he screamed, "Help!" at the top of his lungs and jumped so high the letters flew all over. He saw a green baby snake with a red tongue, trying to crawl up his arm. Frankie turned pale and fled. The inmates burst out laughing, so Frankie threw his shoes at them, but the snake seemed to be crawling on the floor.

"It's just a rubber snake, Frankie. It ain't gonna bite you. Feel it, see?"

"Take it away, take it away! No wonder you have to stay in jail, you mean cotton picker!"

"Oh, Frankie, we like you very much."

"Huh, flattery. I don't like you no more, evermore. Bob, I thought you my friend. Don't just sit there giggling. Do something. Put them all in jail!"

They all burst out laughing. They were happy together, and Frankie loved the crazy gangs more and more.

Peter's Wedding

Frankie also used the newsletter to share his personal experiences – such as his delight in the wedding of his seminary roommate. Peter had asked him to be a groomsman, so Frankie took part in the whole affair.

"Say, this is a fancy coat! I've never worn a tuxedo before. What is this? Cummerbund, huh? Put on my waist? This is neat! Look at me everybody. Handsome?"

"Frankie! Hurry up; you don't have time to play like that."

"Where is my hat, Mom? Anyone sees my shoes?" Frankie asked Peter's mother.

The parsonage was upside down with everyone running upstairs and down, shouting and screaming happily. Peter had six groomsmen from all over – Pennsylvania, Virginia, Florida, South Carolina, and Tokyo, Japan. His older brother, who was a pastor, conducted the wedding ceremony, and his father, also a pastor, gave a short sermon. Frankie was amazed at how many people attended. He had preached at their church a couple years prior to this, so people remembered him, and Frankie suspected that some came just to see him. He said, "I did not tell Peter about it. I just keep my mouth shut, wouldn't you?"

In his delightful way, he greeted many friends outside when suddenly he exclaimed, "Oops! Excuse me. My cummerbund slips down!" He said he was grateful for his suspenders. Frankie loved this Setzer family; they always treated him as one of their own. At the end of that day, Frankie returned to the prison. He was hot and tired but full of joy.[13]

A Peak into the Personality of Frankie San

The newsletter also gave opportunity to describe and share many of the other activities and much of the work that Frankie launched. For instance, in addition to being Santa Claus, Frankie also played the Easter bunny. Imagine a Japanese Easter bunny with floppy ears and a carrot on its tail as it hopped into the hundred-year-old building with its embittered, hateful inmates. Can you imagine the dark, decaying, cellar-like atmosphere and the tension of life with caged men? Then picture a Japanese Easter bunny hopping and laughing and dancing into that area.

In spite of the circumstances, joy, peace, life, and freedom were dispensed along with friendship, pillowcases, and love. Meeting Frankie changed many lives. One inmate said, "His life is a word I've only glimpsed from time to time. His name is Frankie San, and the spirit's name is Jesus Christ and the word is love."[14]

One inmate wrote of Frankie: "I have worked with, cried with, prayed with, and laughed with Frankie San, and I have been a recipient of his love and kindness for eleven years, for I have been here that long." He said Frankie was not simply a gentle little man. Many days he seemed ten feet tall. The anger and frustration of working toward enormous goals and the

---

13   Adapted from excerpts from *Cell 55*, August 1966.
14   Adapted from the newsletter on November 1983.

tremendous pressure that went with it made him cry. Sometimes Frankie even screamed and hollered and threw things at them.[15]

One story that was shared in the newsletter was about a New Year's Eve when Frankie stayed up half the night and morning to prepare a surprise for the fifteen men on death row. He served them a salad with lettuce, tomatoes, pickles, mushrooms, avocados, onions, radishes, oranges, and olives – black and green. The salad also had carrots, cucumbers, bell peppers, and eggs. It was a beautiful salad. But then came the pastries – doughnuts of many flavors – jelly, lemon, coconut, glazed, and chocolate. On the side were pretzels with French bread.

The men on death row loved it. On the first day of that year, they were reminded that someone cared about them and treated them like special people. They all sent him little messages of thanksgiving afterward.[16]

Frankie owned an electric frying pan, and on occasion, as the rumors go, the frying pan would appear on death row for a steak dinner or pancake breakfast. It was an act of love and kindness from God's servant to the least of the castaways.

---

15   Adapted from the newsletter on January 1981.
16   Adapted from the newsletter on January 1981.

Chapter 7

Teaching

Frankie began his teaching career in June 1966 when the South Carolina Department of Corrections hired him as an Adult Education teacher at Central Correctional Institution. Parker Evatt, executive director of the Alston Wilkes Society, thought his friends Ellis MacDougall and Bill Leeke were crazy to hire Frankie San to teach men to read and write when he could hardly speak English. Funds were scarce, so Director MacDougall allowed Frankie to live on campus, eat from the cafeteria, and collect a hundred dollars a month in pay. Two months later, federal monies for vocational training came through and Frankie received an annual salary for his first teaching assignment.

Parker Evatt's uneasiness in hiring Frankie might have been well founded. This foreigner, dressed in his plaid suit and bow tie, was to teach the inmates English through his native Japanese dialect, but this opportunity brought joy to Frankie and he persevered.

"Okay, you guys," he began, "take out first textbook . . . we're all gonna learn Engrish. Yes, I said Engrish. Do I stutter? What?

You cannot read title? So sorry; that is why you are here. Okay, page one of *The Cat in the Hat*." And so he began.

In his humble way, Frankie wrote a note of thanks to Mr. MacDougall:

> "I sincerely appreciate your acceptance of me in this institution. Your generosity and understanding make so much easier my difficult work among inmates. . . . I hope you will let me stay this home for a long time. There is no better home than this for me. I thank you."

Frankie knew he was naïve and didn't know how to deal with these guys, but the inmates were curious about this foreigner. Lots of con games went on, but Frankie credited his three commissioners – Ellis MacDougall, William Leeke, and Parker Evatt – with protecting him when he made mistakes and encouraging him to continue. Frankie quickly learned that if he was to reach any of the men, he'd first have to love them. Once he had their hearts and trust, he could tell them about the Lord.

The Daily Grind

Within a couple months, Frankie recorded that "I have seven dropped-out students now." For the little Japanese man, this was not an acceptable way to face challenges, so he gave them a pep talk. "All right, my friends. I hope you remember what you learned yesterday. But if you forget, you try over and over again. Don't you ever give up. Once you start, you must finish it. This is all life is about and once you stop learning, you are dead. When I came to your country, I did not understand anything, and I used to cry all the time. But one thing, I did not give up my study even when I failed and failed many times. I tried my best with patience. So hang on and I help you."

Then Frankie proceeded to the lessons. "Okay, William, what is five times three? Oh yes, you know it. Same thing like three ice cream cones. How much is it? Yeah, yeah, fifteen cents. As soon as I say ice cream cones, you understand. I don't get it, William."

William did not have a concept of numbers, and some days he wanted to give up. "If I make a mistake again, do I have to count all over? Why do I have to do it so many times, huh? All the other students left already. Why don't you let me go? I know that. If I can't count the numbers, I can't find a job. You try to help me, but I can't do it."

Frankie knew it was difficult for William, but if he was not able to help him, he might never learn to count to a hundred, so Frankie hid his tears when he had to make William stay longer and study harder.

"Now James, how about five times five? Don't you count with your fingers. You've got only 20 fingers, you know. Very soon your baby will say, 'Dad, don't you know five times five?' I want you to answer me like a machine gun. You can kill me or you'll be dropped dead. Here we go. Okay, good. How about this one? Fine, very good. Excellent. Hey, wait a minute. You answer too fast. I give up. See, you can do it. Let's go get ice creams."

He patted their shoulders and they smiled. Frankie said his students just needed a little encouragement, love, and understanding. They finally "broke the surface of frozen sea by themselves." One problem remained. When they finished Frankie's classes, they wanted to stay with him and not advance to a higher class.

Sometimes Frankie heard things like, "Frankie, Mother heard you preaching, and she'd like to meet you. Can you meet her next visiting day?"

"I want you to meet my son. He's five years old."

"I still don't understand you. Why don't you go back to Japan? You must be crazy or something. I wish I had faith like you."

"You must make an awful lot of money on weekends. You work on Saturday and Sunday. You what? You mean you just come on weekends voluntarily? Why? I don't get it."

Many people would tell Frankie, "Frankie, drink and be merry, tomorrow you'll die."

However, Frankie knew what it meant to rejoice to live a spiritual life. He said, "What more do I want in my life? I let them call me crazy. I am a fool for Christ's sake. I can share my joy in Him, but no one takes away this joy from me."[17]

On some of those sweltering summer days, Frankie took his class outside. They sat on the grass beside one of the buildings. What appeared to be a lively discussion was in fact the lessons of the day. The students were happy to be out of the hot, stuffy classroom and engaged in whatever Frankie served up.

After Frankie's first six months, Parker Evatt visited Frankie at the education building of CCI and watched him through a small window in the door as he wrote something on the blackboard. Parker was shocked to see his little friend crying. Tears streamed down his face. This angered Parker, and he wanted to blast into the classroom to straighten out the situation, but decided to wait until the class was over to speak to Frankie alone.

As the prisoners left, he rushed in to ask what was wrong, and Frankie replied that he was doing great. When Parker asked about the crying, Frankie laughed and said that he had been working a long time with one particular student – trying to teach him how to write and spell his name. Finally, the inmate had accomplished that feat, and Frankie's tears were tears of

---

17   Adapted from *The Gospel According to Frankie San*, July 1966.

joy. He said, "I was thanking God for giving me strength and patience to achieve this."[18]

To his fellow instructors, Frankie was a curious phenomenon indeed. They were all dedicated to helping their inmate students, but Frankie's dedication was almost incomprehensible. They noticed that in the classroom he had the patience of Job; he endured frustration and setbacks with a smile and proceeded to encourage slower learners to keep trying.

The secret to Frankie's success might have been that he didn't just respect each student, he loved him as a soul. He wasn't content to teach and go home; he stayed and socialized in the evenings. It was a genuine interest, a healthy concern for the well-being of his friends. He held a class anytime the men wanted to learn, regardless of the number of students.

The other instructors even looked to Frankie for inspiration when they were discouraged. He was a pillar of strength, and his enthusiasm carried all of them. Frankie gave and gave and gave. From his slender hands, he'd offer a bar of soap, a book, a couple stamps. His mouth coached difficult phonetic sounds from illiterate students.

Along with the English and math skills, these inmates learned about the God who loves them. Without God, their chances back on the streets were greatly diminished. As one inmate said, "I have learned it is better to be in prison with Christ than to be on the streets without Him. I know that when I need help in any manner, I can reach up and take His hand. I once tried to lift myself up by my own bootstraps, but in this attempt, I pulled my feet out from under me. By placing my hand in His, I am gently lifted through all trouble and strife. I can depend on Jesus. Prison bars cannot keep Him out. They even let Frankie in."

---

18   Adapted from *Cell 55*, Christmas 1989.

Fruits of the Labor

Frankie's Basic Education for illiterates grew to include prisoners who progressed to the high school level. Graduations with cap and gown became an annual prison affair, and prisoners were given a better chance to succeed once they were outside the walls.

This education was exactly what Charles had needed. He started life without the influence of a mother and father, so he resorted to a life of crime. He stole small items, then cars. He hid out and slept in the woods, cold and hungry. He spent time in reform schools and jails and finally prison. In and out of one facility after another, but finally ending up in Frankie's class where he learned to read and write.

Education is often the key to a man's success beyond those prison walls, and Charles realized that. He said, "I am now taking a trade in prison and with the help of God maybe when I am released this time, I will have something to look forward to. I have learned many things here in the prison school. Whereas if I had been in the free world, I could not have wrote my name. With the trade that I am taking, I feel that I have gained something in life. I hope when I leave here this time, with God's help, I will be a better man and never again return to prison."

Ronnie was an ex-inmate who wrote from beyond the prison walls. He said:

> Well, I'm free, but still in the bonds of Christ.
> Thank you for helping me the first week I was
> out. . . . I have found the value of prayer and
> faith. Without this, I would surely be lost in total
> darkness. Were it not for you, I would still be in
> the dark. From you I learned true and unwav-
> ering faith in God. . . . While I was in the state

penitentiary, I found God. Not the pious, "holier than thou"-type stuff, but one that was real. I found God behind prison bars, and I'm proud of finding an all-loving, all-encompassing God.

One time Frankie expressed his concern over the praise he was receiving. "The inmates' articles always praise me, but we should praise God and not individuals. I can do nothing; only God uses me."

Yes, he was right, but these articles were not the self-praise that Frankie feared. They were praise of God by men who were only beginning to learn about God. Frankie loved them first; then they could realize that Frankie's love was greater than human love. *Greater love has no one than this, that one lay down his life for his friends* (John 15:13). He loved with God's love. When the inmates saw this, they wanted to know more of this God and His love.

But Frankie experienced hard times too. In one newsletter he apologized for not writing sooner and admitted to having difficulties. He said, "My adjustments to the new world have not been easy. It has been a tremendous strain, both physically and mentally, and these were times that I have doubted whether or not I could make it. But always the Lord kept me going."[19]

Hopson

One quality that Frankie San possessed that enabled him to connect with the inmates was his ability to recognize and discover their skills, strengths, and talents. He saw potential in those who could not read or write at an acceptable grade level, and worked with them to bring them to a standard that would allow them to find employment.

---

19   Adapted from an excerpt from *Cell 55*, 1967.

As he addressed their English skills, Frankie discovered that several inmates were particularly adept at writing poetry. So he sponsored a poetry contest with Dr. Reinartz and Dr. Schott, professors at the Lutheran Theological Southern Seminary, to select the winner. First prize went to Hopson for his insightful poem about laughter:

> I wear a cloak of laughter,
>> Lest anyone should see
> My suit of sorrow underneath,
>> And stop to pity me.
>
> I wear a cloak of laughter,
>> Lest anyone should guess
> That what is hid beneath it,
>> Is less than happiness.
>
> But what else does it matter,
>> To you who are so wise,
> My cloak falls tattered at your feet,
>> Before your tender eyes.
>
> Oh, futile cloak of laughter,
>> How frail you are and thin,
> True love looks through so easily
>> And sees the grief within.
>
> I see vast throngs of people
>> But thirst for human cheer:
> My heart's weighed down with loneliness
>> Because you are not near.[20]
>>> – Hopson

---

20   Excerpt from *Cell 55*, November 1966.

Frankie routinely discovered such talent, whether in writing, teaching, or even music, that the inmates possessed. This allowed the men to understand and believe that he cared for and about them.[21]

At the end of a long day of teaching on the way back to his quarters, everything became quiet; stars twinkled in the skies; soft breezes whispered through the leaves. Even the crickets played their instruments joyfully and peacefully. Frankie thanked the Lord, prayed for his brothers, and praised God for His everlasting love and salvation.

"Dear Lord, Jesus Christ, teach me to seek no other way but to find my rest and hope in Thee alone. Thou art the only way. Comfort my suffering brothers and their families in Thee, I pray. Amen."

> *I have been crucified with Christ; and it is no longer*
> *I who live, but Christ lives in me; and the life which*
> *I now live in the flesh I live by faith in the Son of*
> *God, who loved me and gave Himself up for me.*
> (Galatians 2:20)

---

21   Adapted from an excerpt from *Cell 55*, September 1966.

Chapter 8

Raging Riots

Riots of 1968

As encouraging and delightful as the newsletters were, there seems to be a segment of time when they were not written – or were perhaps lost. One can only surmise that it might have been due to riots. The year was 1968, the worst ever for riots, with four different altercations between April and October.

Conditions at the prison fueled much of the anxiety and animosity. The huge granite-and-brick building, which was constructed in 1867, was a five-story, castle-like structure that included several additions. This foreboding medieval fortress was South Carolina's only maximum security prison. Cell Block 1 was the most primitive living area where cells were only five feet wide, six feet deep, and six and a half feet tall, with steel grate doors that were locked with large padlocks. Large roaches crawled around at night, and during thunderstorms the building vibrated as rain and wind penetrated the cracks in the granite blocks.

A "tunnel" was designed to connect all major parts of the prison, but made it one of the hardest prisons to manage. It was not designed to control the inmates' movements or limit their conflicts. Fear was the usual emotion experienced when a person entered the tunnel. Dangers lurked in the shadows of that stretch of hallway. A chapel claimed a space at one end, and inmates' quarters occupied the opposite end.[22]

Inmates thought of the tunnel itself as a "purgatory," a "hell-hole," a walk between "heaven and hell" – a main street of sorts. The smell of sweat and smoke filled the air, and its ceiling vents were pitch-black with dirt and grime, but one had to walk the tunnel to get to the living, working, and eating areas. Unlike a friendly commons area, the tunnel was where inmates went to rumble. Violence would sporadically erupt anytime and anywhere in the tunnel. The confinement of violent offenders in crowded, crumbling units created a volatile situation. Every day was an unknown.

Inmates fashioned pipes into firearms and sharpened spoons to make "shanks" to be used in stabbings. In April 1968, angry convicts rioted for three straight days in the tunnel and out in the yard.

Altogether, in those months of riots, six inmates were killed and sixty-eight were injured. Bill Leeke, the warden who had only been on the job for a few months, addressed the grievances through a bullhorn while standing on a wooden bleacher, surrounded by inmates. In the coming years he was able to establish a psychiatric center and make psychiatrists, psychologists, and social workers available to these men.

But where was Frankie in all of this? Well, Frankie was where he usually was – inside the prison. He had a visiting pastor, Paulwyn Boliek, with him that day. They had gone through the tunnel to the ward where Bobby was quartered. Thirty to forty beds were lined up like a military barracks. Pastor Paul and

---

22   "Columbia Journal: Prison Lures Them In (as Tourists)," *The New York Times National edition*, February 21, 1994, Section A, p. 12.

Bobby sat on Bobby's bed and talked while Frankie wandered through the ward and chatted with the other men.

All of a sudden, they heard frightening noises from the tunnel – loud, cursing voices; splintering wood, and running feet. All of the men in that ward rushed to the barred, iron door to see what was happening. The tunnel was a mass of humanity running back and forth. Chaos ruled and no one was safe. Uniformed guards with billy clubs rushed in to attempt to control the men. The PA system blared, "All inmates return to your quarters . . . All inmates return to your quarters."

Poor Pastor Paul. His fear turned to nausea when he saw blood running down the front of a prison official's suit. An inmate had jerked a fire extinguisher off the wall and smashed it into his face. All of the officers fled to the outside, and the guards slammed the door to the ward – shut and locked, but Frankie and Pastor Paul were still inside. They heard fighting and yelling, then running and clanging of iron doors. They sat on a bed and waited. Bobby and his friends laughed at Frankie and the "preacher" for being locked up. Frankie was calm but his friend was scared. A young inmate sat down by him and said, "Preacher, don't you dare go out there into the tunnel. Some of the men are looking for civilian hostages." That did not help curb the pastor's fear.

Gradually the noise subsided as inmates were herded back to their quarters. After almost an hour, Frankie peered into the tunnel, and a guard told him it was safe to leave. On the way out, the young pastor walked as close to Frankie as he could – through the tunnel, through locked doors, and into the sunshine. Fresh air and freedom never felt so good to him.

Pastor Paul had felt fear while Frankie felt sorrow and grief for what the inmates were doing to themselves. He drew his strength and courage from the Lord because he had already given his life to Him.[23]

Frankie said, "The unexpected prison riot was more violent than I could imagine, and I had been through a war!" In spite of the commotion, he was able to remain calm among angry inmates as officials worked to bring the prison under control.

A Matador Fight

When Barry (not his real name) first met Frankie San, he was awaiting trial for a murder charge. They became close friends immediately, and when Barry was convicted and sentenced to death, Frankie spent many hours visiting him on death row. They often sat on the cement floor on opposite sides of the bars and just talked. Those visits gave Barry much-needed relief from the thoughts of the electric chair in the building next door.

One day Frankie came with his lunch tray, sat on the concrete, and shared his meal with Barry. Frankie could have gone to the officers' dining room and had much tastier food, but he seemed to enjoy eating what his "brothers" ate. All was quiet while they ate, except for the cleaning crew, but all of a sudden, they heard a racket, and Frankie quickly stood up. "Someone is fighting," he said.

When a fight starts in a prison, the only safe thing to do is stay out of the way, so Barry reached through the bars to grab Frankie, but he was too late. The men were already fighting in front of Barry's cell. One guy grabbed Frankie to use him as a shield. The second guy tried to get past Frankie to stab the first one with a homemade knife. He lashed out, and Frankie dodged like a matador fighting a bull.

---

23   "Riots, a bomb and a helicopter escape: 6 big stories from SC prisons," *The State*, April 19, 2018; *www.thestate.com/news/local/crime/article209222199. html*, accessed September 5, 2019.

Barry feared Frankie would not escape that fight without getting hurt, so he closed his eyes to avoid seeing the stabbing of his friend. Then, as fast as it started, it was over. The man behind Frankie had slipped away, and the guards took the other man. Everything settled down – everything except Frankie, that is.

Pale, weak-kneed, and shaking, Frankie went back to Barry's cell. Barry's hands were stiff and sore from gripping the cell bars while his friend was in danger. Both men were somewhat dazed by the danger that had sprung up so quickly. Frankie forced a smile and tried to mask his fear. No doubt he knew how close he had come to death. "Remember, the Lord watches over me; let His will be done," he said.

Barry's death sentence was reduced to life, so his friendship with Frankie had time to grow. He often went to the library, and Frankie helped him face his life sentence.[24]

---

24   Adapted from an excerpt from "A Matador Fight," *Cell 55*, 1978.

Chapter 9

Refuge in a Library

In the summer of 1975, the SCDC chose to open a library at the CCI as part of a program of rehabilitation. Books and furniture were ready; plant containers waited to be placed in appropriate places. The area was to be a resource for information and entertainment for the confined men. One thing was lacking – an individual who could make the library a meaningful contribution to a man's recovery or a brief refuge from the frustrations of prison life. The library needed a heart.

Several men had turned down this opportunity, but Frankie San accepted the new challenge of the position of librarian at CCI, and after a few short months, he was able to say he was thankful for the new door the Lord had opened for him. Instead of teaching a few men in a small classroom, he could see many more men and offer them hope of a better future. Of course, Frankie admitted that the more his mission expanded, the more trouble he got into. He was laughed at and mocked; he was also cursed.

Eventually the library took shape. It became an oasis with the chirp of lovebirds, the gurgle of an aquarium with exotic fish, and the scratching and snuffling of hamsters and rabbits. With miniature Japanese gardens and large fronds of semitropical plants, it could have been a greenhouse. The deep-cushioned, comfortable lounge chairs and a soft sofa made it an escape from the cold, crumbling brick walls of the cells. It didn't look like what it was – a library for prisoners at CCI. The peaceful atmosphere was the result of Frankie San's hard work.[25]

All new inmates toured the library upon their arrival at CCI during their orientation program. They might have been met by a large iguana or the twinkling eyes and flashing smile of a little Japanese man who fed the rabbits and watered the plants. Frankie had a dream of making a place for inmates to relax and for a while forget what they had done. It was a little paradise.

"All the men that come in here have some potential," Frankie said. "Whatever they have done, they are still human beings. As much as I can, I will try to treat them as human beings, not like criminals. I will give them a chance."[26]

Prisoner Antics

The library came to be known as Frankie's domain – he was the boss. It was the most beautiful place in the prison because he made it that way. One inmate related, "All the stupid stuff that you have got in there is a nice mess, and I love it. The birds (Bonnie and Clyde), the fish, the lizards, and all those stuffed animals really make the library a place of peace and quiet that I really like. I can relax in the library; everyone can."

This inmate went on to tell the story of the early days of the aquarium. "Frankie had a garfish in one of his aquariums, and he caught Doug feeding the goldfish to the garfish. Frankie was jumping up and down mad at Doug and made everyone leave the library. Then a couple of days later, Frankie saw a few of the

---

25 Adapted from an excerpt from "CCI Library," by Bill Higgins, *Cell 55*, January 1977.
26 Excerpt from *Cell 55*, January 1977.

goldfish in the tank with the garfish again. He ran over there and was hopping mad until he saw that the prankster had put a rubber band around the garfish's mouth. The joke was on Frankie, and everyone laughed."[27]

Charles had come to the library simply to escape everything. He said he would get stoned in the morning and then go to the library where he could watch a movie or play with the animals. One day he got too loud though. Out of the front office came Frankie with a broom in his hand. This little oriental man started hitting this six-foot-five, 275-pound guy. He chased him right out of the library with that broom, swinging and swatting. Charles laughed, but exited the library, and Frankie's broom gained a reputation.

That was Charles's first "contact" with Frankie. He had heard stories about him – that he was a crazy guy with a big heart, and that he was a master of many kinds of martial arts. Charles did not know what was true except that he was very good with a broom.

Charles stayed away after that, but one day as he was walking past the library, he was hit from behind with a broom. He spun around and there stood Frankie San. He wanted to know why Charles didn't come to the library anymore. Charles said he figured he wasn't welcome, but Frankie told him that was only for one day and this was a new day. Charles was shocked, not only because he was welcomed back but also because Frankie had noticed he was missing amongst the many men who came and went every day.

Charles enjoyed talks with Frankie after that and became one of his volunteers. Frankie exhibited confidence in Charles even when Charles had none of his own. He was so busy in the library and with homework that he did not get high as often. After some time, Charles went to work for Frankie as a

---

27   Adapted from *Cell 55*, Christmas 1990.

law clerk and discovered that he enjoyed helping others with their cases. What began with a misbehaving of an inmate and a broom-thrashing by Frankie led to a man with a purpose to help others.

Opportunities

Many of the men came to the library of their own accord, but others came by personal invitation. In fact, on Christmas Day when Frankie San, as Santa, went from cell to cell handing out the gifts that he had purchased and wrapped, he greeted the men by name. Sometimes he looked at a prisoner and said, "You new man?" If he was, most likely he was wondering what Santa was doing in prison. Then Santa would say, "Come to library if you need help. I help." In this way the library served as a means of connecting and continuing the love that Santa shared.

Prisoners actually felt free in the library rather than imprisoned in a cell. They played games around shiny polished tables, read books, and wrote letters, essays, and poems. Guinea pigs and hamsters ran around in cages, and birds of all kinds perched on swings. Men could sit on the floor, stretch out on pillows, and relax. This little oasis calmed the nerves and tempered the tensions. The books and conversation in a normal room with rugs on the floor provided them with a means of recognizing their worth before God, and they were free to enjoy these peaceful surroundings.

Eventually, Frankie was able to host a delicious Thanksgiving dinner in his library for his workers. Then with satisfied stomachs, they decorated the whole place for Christmas. Frankie's library crew was a family that learned to trust one another and work together.

Early one January, an inmate named Dallas went to the library to see Frankie. He showed him a pencil drawing on an envelope and told him he did not have any materials to draw with. Frankie studied this man. His arms were covered with blue tattoos, his hair was messy, and his clothes were too big and looked shabby. For once, Frankie was hesitant. He had helped two of the toughest guys for a couple months. He knew they were the worst and nobody bothered to mess with them. They were smart, but they were misfits in the joint. Nobody bothered them, so Frankie had challenged them voluntarily. They were "too tough to chew on and they sent me to hell a couple of times. That was a very scary feeling and I failed miserably." Frankie had not recovered from that painful experience yet, but he looked at Dallas. He looked at the drawing again. Dallas was still waiting anxiously.

Finally, Frankie told him he'd buy him a few drawing pencils and a sketch pad the next day. Dallas hesitated, then he said he preferred to paint with brushes and a canvas. Frankie told him he'd have to wait a few days. Dallas thanked him politely and left.

After a few days, Dallas returned to the library, and Frankie gave him the paints, brushes, and canvas. The very next day he brought Frankie his first painting – mentioning that it was still wet. He showed promise so Frankie gave him more canvases and let him paint in the back room. He painted every day all day long. He copied Jesus on the water, the Prodigal Son, several portraits, and lots of scenery. Frankie made suggestions to him about improvements.

Then Frankie purchased an art book for Dallas to learn more about painting, but a few days later another inmate told him that Dallas couldn't read. So the next time that Frankie went to the art store, he asked more questions and discovered some art videos that Dallas could watch to learn more. Dallas watched them all. Then he wanted the special brushes and paints, so Frankie bought those too. Dallas's painting continued to improve until one day he suggested painting a mural on the library wall. Frankie gave him the okay, and he had it done in two days. Truly, the library and Frankie provided the means for Dallas to discover and use his God-given talent.

Another inmate who came to the CCI library was quite the opposite of Dallas. Steve was well educated and had been a successful businessman, but through a series of bad decisions found himself in prison. Frankie hired him as a law clerk, which enabled him to work on his own case and help others also. After Steve had completed his sentence, he asked to stay for a while to continue working on a couple other cases.

But the legal cases were not the only thing that caused Steve to redirect his life. In a note to Frankie, he wrote, "Frankie, most of all I thank you for guiding me and for not letting me run away. I have learned more from you in one week that I have ever learned in such a short time before. For the caring and love you have showered upon me I can never repay you, only offer in return my love to you, and in hopes that someday I can pass that on to another who may need the caring and love to help them through a hard time." Such words carried more strength than anything Frankie could have said about himself, for Scripture tells us to *let another praise you, and not your own mouth; a stranger, and not your own lips* (Proverbs 27:2).

The library offered an opportunity for Frankie to invite some inmates to work for him. The law library in particular gave men a reason to get up in the morning. Their days had purpose. The time they spent in the library was also time spent with Frankie. Lengthy conversations allowed them to relate on a personal level, and he listened, offered advice, and encouraged them.

One inmate, Tom, found his way to the library soon after entering CCI. He was a voracious reader and picked up a new book every day. But because the rules only allowed him to check one book out at a time, he often put a second one, sometimes a third, in the back of his pants under his coat. By the next day, though, he would have read those books and needed more. Tom enjoyed his time in the library. Something about that place made him feel good, so he finally asked Frankie if he could do some kind of work for him – typing, filing cards, or anything else to fill his days. After ten months, he worked full-time in the library and enjoyed what he was doing.

Then the Department of Corrections decided that the library staff should make special trips to the segregated units at least twice a week to deliver books. Tom argued that the men in those areas were there for punishment or they were seeking protective custody because they owed a drug dealer or had testified against someone. Tom's objections fell on deaf ears. Frankie simply started to deliver books, and after six months, they delivered over eight hundred books each month while making three thousand individual visits with the inmates in those units. The books provided more access to the men who needed to be treated as human beings.

Then Frankie came up with the idea of collecting used paperback books from his friends in the churches and surrounding areas. By doing this, they were able to add many more books to those already in the library. More and more inmates read books as more were available. Tom noticed that some of the books were misplaced or carried away, never to be seen again. He kept telling Frankie that they were going to lose all their books. Frankie said, "Books . . . books don't matter . . . they can be replaced . . . we must give these men something to do and feed their minds." In the end, Frankie was right. Every time Tom complained about more books disappearing, they would get another small box or sack with more paperbacks from a church or friend.

After the book distribution was established, Frankie purchased a color television and video recorder to establish a movie room in the library. Every day 150 to 200 inmates flocked in to watch movies, which might have been their only enjoyment of the day. This rough bunch giggled, laughed, clapped, and screamed through some of the movies. Even with the overcrowded conditions, they were well behaved. Tensions and anxieties were relieved, and for a time they escaped the harsh realities of their lives. Sometimes as Frankie stood back and watched the inmates, tears rolled down his cheeks, and he would leave the library. How he wanted to get his men a projector television for these movie times, so they would be able to see the screen better.

The New Television

In 1981 Frankie had the opportunity to return to Japan to visit his parents. He had not been back for sixteen years, so the reunion was a delightful time. When the excitement died down, Frankie's thoughts returned to his brothers in prison and their needs. He talked to his younger brother, Tadamasa, about purchasing a large-screen television for the library. The cost, however, was beyond his means, so Frankie hoped that the Sony company in Japan would donate one to the prison.

Tadamasa called a politician friend, Tanaka San, and a few days later he came to visit Frankie. Frankie's hopes were high, but Tanaka San told him that an executive suggested he write to the Sony company in New York. Disappointed that he did not have the television to take back with him, he waited until he returned to America. Then he wrote a long letter to the New York Sony company, hoping for a donated television. However, they replied that they had already donated as many as they were allotted; there were none left for prisoners. More disappointment.

Frankie soon learned that Sony planned to build a plant on the outskirts of Columbia, and a representative would be in the area. All those involved with the plant were optimistic – that is, until inflation increased so much that Sony chose to postpone the project. More disappointment.

In the midst of all that frustration, the library's little television died. Frankie took it to the repair shop, but they told him it would cost two hundred dollars to fix, which was too much money for that old set. He decided to buy a new one the same size. While looking for the small television, he discovered that a large fifty-inch television had dropped to half the original price – but even at that, it was too much. Christmas was coming and Frankie needed that money. Besides, Frankie's parents wanted him to return one more time before they passed away. Frankie just did not have the money for the big-screen television.

Giving up was not in Frankie's genes however. As he traveled out of town, he stopped at television shops. He stopped at Walmart. He stopped at Sam's Club. He had half the money that he needed but couldn't see how he could come up with the rest. As he drove toward home one night, he suddenly experienced the peace and joy of God in an overwhelming way. He rejoiced because he knew he should not worry about the money. The next day Frankie received a check from Minneapolis; a few days later one came from a friend, and a church in Columbia also sent a check. Frankie ordered the television, and it was delivered and installed a few days before his birthday – a gift from the Lord to Frankie and the prisoners.[28]

Men Helping Men

Not only did Frankie invite men to the library, but some of his workers and volunteers also invited others. One day Joe invited Randy to work as a volunteer. Though Randy did not think the library was the place for him, he went to talk to Frankie. In

---

28   Adapted from *Cell 55*, Christmas 1983.

a few months, Randy said he felt something changing inside him – his attitude. He enjoyed the daily chores that Frankie gave him, but the time in conversation was the best. It helped him understand he needed spiritual growth.

Randy sometimes helped Frankie deliver books to the men in lockup; he saw men spit on Frankie and scream obscenities. When Randy asked how he could take so much abuse, Frankie said, "Randy, that is what they did to Jesus. They spat on Him and called Him names and finally crucified Him. God chose me to do this most important work, and I must follow Him whatever the cost." With that, Randy declared that for the first time in a long time he felt a little joy creeping back into his life.

When Randy's family and their pastor came to visit, several of the inmates cleaned the library until it was spotless. Frankie purchased drinks, paper plates, spoons, and forks. The guys were excited, and all sensed that something special was happening. God was at work that day. The inmates welcomed the guests with respect – no profanity and no obscene gestures. Joy filled the air as the gospel was shared. Such a lively time of conversation followed that the feeling of family filled the library. For a time, they were family. Men helping men in the prison.

Improvements

One would think that law books might be the last thing in the world that inmates might want, but some of these men were quite educated and wanted to study law. Even those who were not educated needed to understand how the law worked. Some desired to appeal their own cases or help others understand how to do that. Some even managed to earn law degrees. Law books, however, like most academic books, were expensive. One inmate, Harry, worked continuously to improve the law library at CCI. He kept telling Frankie, "We need more and better law books."

One month a Christian television film crew came to the facility to do a documentary about the conditions at the prison and its problems. One of the interviewers spent three days with Frankie and several inmates. At the end of that time, she asked what they needed in the library. Immediately, Frankie told her that they desperately needed a particular set of law books. Frankie often solicited donations for the needs of the inmates. He had learned from Scripture that *you do not have because you do not ask. You ask and do not receive, because you ask with wrong motives* (James 4:2-3). Frankie's motives were pure and righteous. The interviewer smiled; then she said, "In the name of the Lord, we will donate those books." Once again, God provided for these castaway men.

The Heart of the Library

Yes, the library needed heart, and when Frankie San accepted the position, the library gained a beating heart of love and compassion. Even to the casual observer, the CCI library spoke of Frankie. His personality permeated throughout, and his character curbed misbehavior. The library was a reflection of Frankie – who was a reflection of Christ Himself.

Inmates felt as though they were sitting in Frankie's own living room when they spent time in the library. They were guests. They could sit in a home atmosphere like they might never have had before. This took the men out of the prison environment and mentality for a short time and reminded them of their own humanity.

Chapter 10

Christmases in Confinement

Frankie's First Christmas behind Bars

Frankie had made the commitment to live within the prison when he began his ministry behind the walls. That first Christmas he could have reveled and partied with others in their homes, but he thought it would be best to share that day with the inmates and gain a sense of what they experienced. Behind those walls, he witnessed the bleakness that reigned in the cells.

Men without families reflected a special emptiness. The thick, cold granite and dull, grey cement told nothing of the bright, warm Christmas reds and greens. No Christmas tree, no bright lights, and no joyful laughter. Every day was a carbon copy of every other day, and the birthday of Jesus passed as any other.

Frankie, frail and barely acquainted with his mission, spent that day wandering behind the high walls, quietly observing the ugly faces and shuffling feet of men a million miles from Christmas. Down the long, damp tunnel, across the windy yard, through the hospital and psychiatric cellblock he roamed. Everywhere, the same gloom and doom hung in the air.

He wondered how such sadness and despair could exist in that facility when just a few miles away in downtown Columbia, bright lights twinkled and the joyful warmth of the Christmas spirit filled every corner. He knew he could have joined the cheer, but he needed to be inside the walls. He believed the shepherd's place is with his flock, and if he were to ever understand the bitterness and sorrow of each prisoner, he had to live with the outcasts and share their miseries.

Late that afternoon he spoke quietly with the condemned men on death row. Then he visited with the individuals locked down in the "hole." As the sun set, he passed through the steel jaws of the front gate and went to his tiny room. Lonely and isolated, he meditated about the day that had marked the saddest Christmas in his life. Tears tumbled down his cheeks as the crushing sorrow squeezed his chest. Silently, he prayed for Christ to help him bring Christmas behind those walls.

Each Christmas thereafter saw an increase in answers to his prayer. For the second Christmas Frankie acquired boxes of used Christmas cards from his friends in the "free world" and showed the prisoners how to remake them into "new" useable cards. That year hundreds of prisoners sent Christmas cards. On Christmas Day, he organized a songfest with a couple guitars and some borrowed booklets of Christmas carols. The time was a great success, with lots of participation and interest.

Encouraged by the results, Frankie expanded the card project and began the "soap project" the following year. By December 25, he had purchased and scrounged enough soap for every man in the prison hospital, on death row, and in the psychiatric cellblock. With each bar of soap, he added a personal Christmas message about Jesus. He lit a light within the dark prison walls that caused the men to respond and even reflect that light.

Each year the response grew and he worked harder and

harder to bring joy and earn their trust. As the work mounted up, he decided to enlist the aid of his fellow Christians beyond the walls. He took the Christmas project and plight of his imprisoned brothers to his friends in the free world. With the responses he received, he was able to reach out to more inmates with small gifts.

Spending that first Christmas in the sorrow and sadness behind the walls had burdened Frankie's heart, but it also caused him to pray for his confined brothers. With each passing year, God answered his prayer to bring light and joy to those trapped in that darkness.[29]

The Penitentiary – His Bethlehem

Frankie San put great importance on the Christmas holiday. One might wonder, did he regard that day with too much significance? Is not one day the same as the next? The apostle Paul tells us in Romans 14:5, *One person regards one day above another, another regards every day alike. Each person must be fully convinced in his own mind.*

But Frankie felt a special connection with the story of the birth of Christ. He recognized that the lowly, poor shepherds must have been surprised when they found the Christ child in a manger among the cows and horses. Yet he noted that the Bible makes no indication that there was any bitterness in the heart of Mary and Joseph because of this. He knew the innkeeper was not to be blamed, for it was a busy time with the taxes due, and many had journeyed to fulfill their obligation. The innkeeper kindly offered the only lodging that was left – the comfort and protection of the stable, and Joseph was grateful. If the babe had been born in a palace, the simple shepherds would not have been able to reach Him.

---

29   Adapted from "The Japanese Santa Claus," *Cell 55.*

Frankie knew God planned this; He manifested Himself in a strange way and a strange place, and the miracle story of His love lives on. *For God so loved the world, that He gave His only begotten Son* (John 3:16). When God's message of peace reached Frankie's heart, he left his native land and, like the lowly shepherds who followed angel voices, said, "Lord, where is the manger you spoke about? Where can I find your peace?"

Frankie answered God's call to the penitentiary. Like the manger setting, he did not find men with prestige and titles. He found common men chained with yesterday's calamities whose lips flowed with unholy words. Strange, but Frankie's Bethlehem was found in the hearts of the inmates. He had no gold, frankincense, or myrrh like the wise men, but he offered his life with the love of his heart. As that love flowed from him, he boldly proclaimed with the shepherds the good tidings that "Christ is born today."

Feeling like a lowly shepherd caused Frankie to celebrate at Christmastime and help all of his brothers in prison to understand the miracle of God being born a man in a manger.[30]

Christmas with Frankie San

One December in the early years of Frankie's service at the prison, Joe assisted Frankie as they distributed thousands of Christmas cards, hundreds of bars of soap, many towels and washcloths, drinking cups, and a multitude of toothbrushes and tubes of toothpaste. Frankie's many generous friends had sent these items for the inmates of the SCDC.

Joe and Frankie loaded the bags and boxes onto a pushcart and proceeded into the various living quarters of the prison. They first entered Building No. 1, a five-tiered building where

---

30   Adapted from "The Penitentiary – My Bethlehem," by Frankie San, *Cell 55*, December 1967.

five hundred men lived. Eager faces greeted them, and men stretched their hands through the heavy iron doors that were set in stone. Somewhere down the line they passed the word: "Here comes Frankie, and he's giving something away!"

"What is it?" someone asked.

"It looks like stamped envelopes."

"Hey, it's Christmas cards!"

"Frankie, over here. Don't forget me."

"Mac, you watch the cards while we go up and give them out," Frankie instructed. "Bill, you and Joe go down that side and I'll get this side." So Bill and Joe loaded themselves up with Christmas cards and climbed the stairs.

"What's this?" demanded a suspicious inmate.

"Christmas cards from Frankie," Bill replied.

The inmate's face broke into a big, toothy grin. "Oh," he said, "oh yeah, thanks. Yeah, thanks a lot."

Frankie and his helpers moved on to Cell Block 2, which housed the death row inmates and state hospital patients. The twelve death row inmates who were housed in that maximum security section of the prison received the gifts with warmth and appreciation and made Frankie's helpers feel good about what they were doing. The inmates' faces usually reflected a perpetual sadness, but on this day, happiness was evident. The "forgotten men" in this cellblock had been remembered.

Later, Frankie and Bill sat on Bill's bed, resting, when someone came and said, "There is a man in one cellblock who hasn't had a visit or a letter in ten years."

That was all it took for Frankie and Bill to gather several gifts and take off. They handed him the gifts, and he said, "For me?" The small gifts were able to touch the man's heart.[31]

---

31   Adapted from "Christmas with Frankie San," *Cell 55*, December 1967.

Here Comes Santa

The role of Santa began with preparations in September. Each weekday afternoon, as soon as Frankie had dismissed his students from Basic Education, he scurried around to assemble and wrap Christmas gifts for nearly three thousand inmates. Into each gift would go some soap, candy, fruit, a coffee cup, and sometimes a towel or a pair of socks.

After five years of serving the men in the correctional institution, Frankie continued to encourage outsiders to remember the forgotten ones who had no one and nothing. Along with the usual plans for the men at the prison, he decided to change things a bit.

Many of the men had been teasing Frankie that since he was their Santa Claus, he should look the part. Several inmates chided him about it until he threw up his hands and said, "Okay, okay, I put red clothes and white whiskers on. You guys gonna drive me nuts!"

Many of them had even forgotten about the colorful Santa pageant but yearned for the joy and sparkle. So Frankie searched for a Santa outfit, which they did not have in Japan. He even called up to Virginia to a dear friend to ask for help. After checking the nearby department stores, Frankie wandered in to an exclusive men's store and related his problem. The owner was amused at this Japanese missionary who needed a Santa outfit to wear in a prison. He offered to make the suit for Frankie at a reasonable price, which delighted Frankie because he did not have the money for an expensive suit.

The next afternoon he went barreling down the tunnel with a check in hand. At the last minute, unexpected funds had come in and Frankie exclaimed with glee, "Just came from a friend in Virginia. Will pay for the Santa Claus suit. How you like those apples?"

But Frankie had no beard and wig and no money for them. The prisoners heard about his problem and planned a solution. They took up a collection and ordered a wig and beard from New York which became his treasure.[32]

So, in 1970, for the first time ever, a "young, handsome, 120-pound Santa Claus" toted his large sack and made rounds at the prison, and America received its first visit from the "Japanese Santa." Singing the little tune, "You better watch out, better be swell, or Santa Claus won't visit your cell," Frankie spread joy and happiness amidst the sorrow and heartaches. Upon entering the huge Cell Block 1, he was greeted by a spontaneous roar from the five hundred residents. Amid laughter, catcalls, whistling, and wisecracks, he visited the cells where he dispensed a small gift, a friendly handshake, and words of cheer through each set of thick bars. After finishing in Cell Block 1, he proceeded to the hospital, psychiatric cellblock, death row, and deadlock, which is prolonged solitary confinement. At midnight he went to one of the wards to conduct caroling and recite the Christmas story. With an empty sack but a brimming heart, the weary Santa returned to his small living quarters, pulled off his boots, and dropped off to sleep, exhausted.

Taking Christmas to Florence School for Boys

After several years of celebrating Christmas at CCI, Frankie and Parker Evatt had received an invitation to bring some cheer to two hundred of the toughest, most incorrigible boys in the state. On the way, Parker had tried to explain to Frankie what it meant to "use your common sense." The language barrier still produced problems.

When they arrived, their friend Chaplain James Pilgrim met them. Frankie asked him if Santa was supposed to come

---

32   Adapted from "A Christmas Story," by Frankie San, *Cell 55*, 1975.

out before or after the refreshments. The chaplain replied, "Frankie, that is your cup of tea." What a puzzled look appeared on Frankie's face, and Parker knew he'd be explaining more English to him on the way home.

Though it was a cold, rainy night, a high school band had come to the gymnasium of the correctional school to provide music, and churches in the area had baked and donated homemade cookies. Through the efforts of the Alston Wilkes Society and Frankie San, gifts had been collected for all of the boys.

The boys filled their plates to overflowing with frosted, decorated cookies and sweets. They took their punch and listened to the music but soon became restless. Parker explained that cookies and music were fine, but it couldn't be a Christmas party without Santa Claus. One boy popped up and said, "I bet he won't be a black Santa Claus."

Parker replied, "You're right, but he isn't a white Santa Claus either!" The boy's eyes opened wide with surprise when Parker told him he'd probably be the smallest Santa Claus he'd ever seen, but he had the biggest heart. "The only way to get this Santa to appear is to sing 'Jingle Bells.'" With that, they nearly brought down the roof as they sang and the band played.

Frankie popped out from the stage curtain, jumped down, and started dancing around the gym floor with a sack on his back. The boys went wild. Everyone laughed at this funny-looking Japanese Santa Claus. After the laughs and hilarity of the Japanese Santa, the boys settled back on the bleachers. Frankie, in his red-and-white Santa suit with a snow-white beard, told about the first Christmas. He read the story from the Bible and then told them about his Christmases when he was a boy in Tokyo. He said, "My mother told me that someday I would grow up to be someone special – and it's true. I'm Santa."

To finish the evening, they turned the lights in the gym off, and Frankie stood with one lone candle. He told them he was not like the Santa Clauses on the street corners; he pulled out the cross that he always wore and said, "I am Santa Claus for Jesus Christ." The boys were so still, a person could have heard a pin drop. Frankie then sang "Silent Night" in Japanese. As he began, the boys spontaneously hummed along, creating a worshipful ending to the evening.

As the boys left the gym, Santa gave each of them several gifts. He received smiles in return but was saddened when he heard many of them say it was the best Christmas they ever had. Frankie determined to do this every year for the boys – which he did.

Christmas Grows and Grows

One year, Kaori, Frankie's niece, joined the incarcerated Santa and his other volunteers to distribute gifts throughout the worst parts of the prison. She shocked the men when they saw her, so they quickly tried to clothe themselves. Some were too slow, but they all stood with their mouths open and whispered, "What in the world is a twelve-year-old girl doing here, visiting us in this filthy place?"

Of course, they were surprised to learn that she was nineteen and a freshman at Columbia College. She proved herself to be quite the lady by ignoring the tattoos and half-naked men while she sang and danced with Santa. Two crazy Japanese characters got everyone's attention with their jitterbugging and music. Cursing came to a halt, smiles broke out, and for a while, laughter echoed throughout the building.

With each passing year, the Christmas project grew. In 1975, Frankie and his supporters were able to share gifts with the Greenville Release Center inmates, the South Carolina State Hospital inmates, the elderly people's home, 700 juvenile delinquents, needy children, 700 new prison inmates, and the 1,800 inmates at the Columbia prison. All of those gifts took much planning and organizing. Frankie ordered 3,000 cups, 2,400 towels, 2,400 pairs of socks, 500 pounds of candy, 200 handballs, and 240 jars of coffee. The cups arrived on December 16 and the socks arrived on the 22nd, but the towels were nowhere to be found. Supposedly, they were in a warehouse in Columbia, but Frankie could not find them. Finally, on December 29, Frankie located the towels – ten huge boxes of them – right in their own visitors' room. For three days Frankie scurried around delivering the towels.

That year was the best Christmas party they had ever had. Ninety maximum security inmates, the toughest, most troublesome men in the prison, took part. For the first time, even the warden and custodial officers participated with two ladies who joined the group. Some asked if this wasn't dangerous, but Frankie said, "Surely not; our Lord was with us."

The inmate band played exciting music, and prisoners shouted joyfully until the ceiling seemed to shake. One of the ladies sang a song of love, and enthusiastic voices rang throughout the building. Then the jolly lady and Santa did the "Jingle Bell Bump" and almost made the walls tumble down. What fun! The officers were bewildered to see hardened criminals behave so normally, but Frankie declared, "Man's sin had separated the kept from the keepers; our Lord's love made us all one on that night."

The darkest dungeon turned into the brightest spot that night. Killers, rapists, thieves – they may have been, but on this Christmas Eve, each felt the beauty of Christmas, and hearts were touched by our Lord. Frankie referred to the apostle Paul when describing what happened:

> *Now I want you to know, brethren, that my circumstances have turned out for the greater progress of*

the gospel, so that my imprisonment in the cause
of Christ has become well known throughout the
whole praetorian guard and to everyone else.
(Philippians 1:12-13)

Last CCI Christmas

Frankie often asked inmates to share their life stories in writing for him and for a record of the lives in prison. One of those prisoners, Charlie, chose not to write about all of his mistakes, but rather to describe that last Christmas behind the walls of CCI. Yes, Charlie was in prison for his crimes despite having had a wonderful life with his wife and daughter. He admitted that he was searching for peace and happiness. Ironically, he found both in prison.

Charlie found his peace when he turned his life over to the One who could give him the assurance that his life had a purpose. The peace came through Jesus Christ, his Lord and Savior. So, instead of writing of his mistakes, Charlie wrote about the blessings that he received within the prison walls.

One of the greater blessings for Charlie was their very own Santa Claus who had become a father to many of the inmates and a friend to all. When Charlie wrote about Frankie, the closing of the prison was near, and this was to be their last Christmas within those walls. So Frankie wanted it to be the best of all Christmases.

Charlie helped Frankie with this celebration. First, they prepared the gifts. They had more than thirteen hundred gifts for the inmates at CCI. He gave each one a pair of socks, a pillowcase, a clothes hanger, an ink pen, and a bag of candy. Of course, that did not include all of the miscellaneous articles he provided throughout the year. Typically, Frankie spent over half of his paycheck to supply the prisoners with what they needed.

Because this grand finale of CCI Christmases was to be recorded, arrangements were made with the cameraman to do this a week before Christmas. Frankie started down the tunnel, clad in his Santa garb and fully equipped with jingling bells. Charlie and nine other inmates, sporting Christmas shirts and hats, served as Santa's helpers. Some of these helpers rode various forms of wheeled mechanisms – a skate bicycle with no front tire, a skateboard, a twelve-inch bicycle, and a scooter. Another had possession of a remote-control truck, and of course, Barney, the library parrot, came along. The rest of the helpers pushed buggies full of gifts.

Frankie cranked up the music on his cassette player and led the Christmas circus parade down the tunnel. He danced in his Santa suit, and his helpers joined in the fun. Ralph, a former professional football player, danced with Frankie – though being six foot four and 240 pounds, light-footed he was not. When Santa passed between the giant's legs, the guys went so wild with laughter that the building seemed to shake.

Even the officers were caught up in the excitement and wanted to ride the bike and run the remote-controlled truck. One could say that Frankie had caused a Christmas riot; this went on the whole time they passed out gifts, which took two evenings. Santa and his helpers were exhausted but joyful when they finished.

This Santa also worked to insure that the families of his library workers were cared for. He sent money to a church where he had preached earlier in the year. He asked them to provide gifts for Charlie's family and they certainly did. They bought gifts for his wife, his daughter, and his mother. The Sunday before Christmas, about fifteen people showed up at the wife's door. They brought the gifts and put them under the tree, along with food for Christmas dinner. Charlie's daughter got the bicycle she wanted, two new outfits to wear, and a baby doll.

Charlie's was only one of the families that Frankie blessed out of the love he had for all men, giving of himself freely all of the time. Frankie helped Charlie find the peace and happiness he sought, as he understood the message of the angel that spoke to the shepherds on that first Christmas. *Behold, I bring you good news of great joy which will be for all the people* (Luke 2:10).

In finishing the article, Charlie said, "I know that the love people have for others would not be possible if our Christ had not been born some two thousand years ago in the manger. He taught us to love, and then He laid down His life for us that we might have life and have it more abundantly."

So the last CCI Christmas blessed many inmates and families. The first Christmas brought the Savior to fallen mankind. *I have come as Light into the world, so that everyone who believes in Me will not remain in darkness* (John 12:46).

Why Such an Emphasis on Christmas?

Surely, Frankie knew the Christian life is much more than celebrating Christmas with Santa and gifts. Most certainly, he wanted more for these men – his brothers. But one inmate on death row, Stephen, related to Frankie what Christmas was to them. He wrote:

> While the holiday season is such an incredible source of great joy for many people, it can actually be the opposite for some. On Death Row the joy of Christmas can become a reminder of loss and pain. As early as Halloween, the atmosphere on Death Row – which is already dismal and gloomy – begins to take on an even more depressing and

gray appearance. The level of despair rises to heights far greater than normal. The simple fact, the basic truth, is that Death Row is comprised of men all sentenced to death, awaiting execution, and trying to do so in the best way possible. The holiday season brings a continuous onslaught of music, commercials, television shows, advertising, and imaging that represents family gatherings and the love of family and friends. As an inmate on Death Row, each and every one of those ads, each image, each symbol, can be a sharp reminder of his and the victims' loss. The pain can grow with each day to incredible lengths.[33]

Why did Frankie spend weeks and weeks preparing the gifts, then dressing like Santa to bring some light-hearted joy to these criminals? He knew that each one of them had been created in the image of God and each one needed to see the love of our Lord. He knew they needed to see someone care for them before their hearts would soften to receive the One who would save them. He loved them with the love of our Lord and labored to make that love known.

> The love of God is greater far,
>   Than tongue or pen can ever tell.
> It goes beyond the highest star,
>   And reaches to the lowest hell.[34]

> "Christmas is not just yesterday or today. Let us not spend Christmas. Let us keep it in our hearts every day throughout the coming year!" – Frankie San

---

33 Excerpt from "The Mask," by Dr. Edward Carney.
34 Frederick M. Lehman, "The Love of God," 1917.

Chapter 11

Felons for Friends

"Learning to love is what makes us human; learning to give ourselves away to others is what makes us really alive." – Frankie San

The company a person keeps speaks of who the person is and what is in his heart. What can be assumed of a man who keeps company with prisoners and felons? Scripture is clear that *bad company corrupts good morals* (1 Corinthians 15:33). But does that mean the castaways in prison are to be shunned? Jesus said, *I was hungry, and you gave Me something to eat; I was thirsty, and you gave Me something to drink; I was a stranger, and you invited Me in; naked, and you clothed Me; I was sick, and you visited Me; I was in prison, and you came to Me. Truly I say to you, to the extent that you did it to one of these brothers of Mine, even the least of them, you did it to Me* (Matthew 25:35-36, 40).

Those are the words that Frankie San lived by as he chose to be a friend to the friendless. Though he knew that the friend who sticks closer than a brother is Jesus Christ, he also knew that these men needed to touch, see, and feel the love from such a friend. He became that walking, living model of Christ for these men to touch and see.

Frankie declared that it was impossible for him to express the joy and peace he experienced each day as he went to work. The Lord gave him joy through the inmates even when they did not understand the crazy Japanese man. But they cared about him. When two inmates discovered he had given his last watch away and had to carry a large alarm clock around, they bought him a beautiful golden pocket watch for his birthday. The golden chain hung from his vest pocket, and he declared it made him feel like a distinguished man.

Frankie made friends in his classes. They were eager learners, so Frankie had to study harder and harder until late at night. He had to learn many new words, which were difficult with his Japanese accent – words like *parallelogram*, *trapezoid*, and *circumference*. He told his students, "You must memorize the value of pi – no, no, you cannot eat this pi, John."

Sometimes he reprimanded them. "Julian, I told you to be in class on time."

"What? You can't wait? You act like a kindergartener! Go ahead."

Sometimes he claimed his students "acted like popcorn on the hot stove," and he "couldn't hold the cover on the pan." Occasionally, he blew his stack because of their misbehavior and "chewed them up." He could never tell what would happen from one moment to the next, but yet they were friends.

After one inmate misbehaved, he came back and said, "Frankie, I'm sorry for what I've done. I won't do it anymore. You have been so good."

Frankie held the guy's head in his arms and thanked the Lord for His steadfast love. A big tear fell on his cheek because he knew that God's love could reach these hungry souls little by little.

"Frankie, are you still mad at me? . . . Oh, you're not! Here, I brought you three apples."[35]

These moments brought joy to Frankie – moments when the inmates, his friends, returned the love of God to him. It indicated to Frankie that they could feel God's love and discipline, and it caused Frankie to love them as his own boys. Their own words help us understand better the effect he had on them. Shortly before being executed, one inmate wrote to Frankie: "Sometimes I have a hard time saying what I'm trying to say, but I believe what I want to say is I love and appreciate you so much. I can't wait for the day when I'm able to spend eternity with you in the presence of our mighty Lord."

They called him the "Little Giant" – small in stature, large in heart. "He cheers us up when we feel as though we are about to come apart at the seams. He offers us a friendly smile and soothing words whenever he sees that we are in need of them. If we are sad and worried and go to Frankie, our problems become his problems, and through misty eyes he tries to offer the correct solution."[36]

Mary

Even before Frankie had his permanent position in the penitentiary, the love that emanated from him endeared him to all who came to know him. When he worked at the Children's Home, he worked with Mary. (Just to be clear – Mary was not a felon.) Until she met Frankie, she had little or no thought of men in the criminal world because she had been sheltered from the horrors of crime in her Christian family. Frankie, however,

---

35   Adapted from an excerpt from *Cell 55*, November 1966.
36   Excerpt from *Cell 55*, 1967.

realized these men needed someone to show them the way. A daily acquaintance with one who walked so closely with God intrigued Mary so much that she wanted to see him in his new work and way of life at the prison.

After Frankie went back to work with the inmates, friends asked Mary where she'd spend her vacation. She told them, "at the penitentiary." They were puzzled, but she had decided to visit Frankie where he lived – in the prison with the inmates. He wanted to identify himself with their hopes, dreams, and fears in order to better understand and help them, and she wanted to experience that part of her friend's life.

As Mary and her husband approached the South Carolina penitentiary, they saw high walls with entangled razor wire surrounding the entire facility and stately guards at strategic vantage points. Big electric doors swung open for them to enter and then clanged shut behind them. A guard ushered them into a waiting room, and soon Frankie appeared. Mary remarked, "His smile was more radiant than the sunshine, and his jet-black eyes twinkled with delight."

Inmates prepared and served lunch for them as they visited with Frankie, but then he had a class scheduled, so Mary toured the facility and had the privilege of meeting Bob, one of Frankie's inmate friends. They visited for almost two hours, while Mary's husband went with Frankie through the penitentiary. The respect and admiration the prisoners had for Frankie was obvious as they called out to him:

"Hey, Frankie, nice to see you."

"Come over here, Frankie. What do you think of this letter?"

"Who is your friend, Frankie?"

Frankie answered each man as questions came from every direction. Such an example of warmth, serenity, and trust is seldom seen – even outside the walls. Love radiated from the young Japanese man as he walked through the tunnel with Mary's husband. They enjoyed a delicious dinner at a fine restaurant that evening with engaging stories and news.

When the day was over, they returned Frankie to the penitentiary; it was dark and still. They hated to leave Frankie, but they knew he was happy. He had a joy that grew out of harmonious, loving relationships with his brothers that was based on tolerance, understanding, and love. He waved to them in the distance, then turned and disappeared into the prison.[37]

Bob

Mary did not consider Bob a complete stranger as she visited with him, for she had helped him in correspondence pertaining to his parole. He had become Frankie's friend even before Frankie left for the Children's Home, and though he tried to reject Frankie and God's love, he couldn't ignore that kind of love. He knew it was his only hope; Frankie's love softened that hard heart and guided him to a saving faith in Christ.

When talking about the possibility of parole, Bob said, "I try to be most optimistic in my outlook and will be keenly disappointed if I am turned down, but I occasionally think that it could be gratifying to be denied parole just so I would have the opportunity to prove that my faith is built on the firm foundation of Christ. No hardship on earth can ever again affect my basic beliefs or future actions. My greatest concern is Frankie's disappointment if I am denied."

When Bob went up for parole in 1965, Frankie was there. When parole wasn't granted, Bob was indeed disappointed – and

---

37   Adapted from an excerpt by Mary "K" Hansbrough from *Cell 55*, September 1966.

bitter, but Frankie did what no one else would have done. He cared so much that he wept. Frankie loved these men, and they marveled at how much love could come from such a little man.

Bob's affection and appreciation for Frankie was evident in his anxiety of causing his friend heartache. He had become a new creature by the Holy Spirit through Frankie, and the two of them remained fast friends.[38] Bob wrote of his conversion in a free-verse poem, "Deluge":

> Though I find myself submerged
> In a swiftly flowing stream;
> Though stout branches of trees
> Overhead offer themselves invitingly,
> I am unable to drink of life
> Or grasp a branch that I may remove
> This self, this mind, this soul
> From the quagmire of my unconsciousness
> As in a dream, my voice is unheard though I shout,
> Beseeching unknown powers that be,
> To give purpose, if ever so fleeting,
> To such aimless flotsam.
> Until someone says, "See!
> The Carpenter has built a raft."[39]

Bob learned from Frankie that it is our task to point men who are floating in life's river of despair to the raft of our salvation that is built by the Lord Jesus. His conversion had connected him with Frankie – closer than brothers.

Bob used his literary skills to teach and point others to the same Savior that Frankie introduced him to – the Lord Jesus Christ. He wrote a poem to Frankie to show him how much

---

38   Adapted from an excerpt by Mary "K" Hansbrough from *Cell 55*, September 1966.
39   Excerpt from *Cell 55*, November 1966.

he meant to the inmates. In this poem, Frankie is the shining ship, and Jesus Christ is the navigator. The isolated men could be anyone, but more specifically, Bob placed them on desert isles because Frankie ministered to the castaways. The ship is borne on the ocean of God's love that washes but is usually ignored, so it retreats and then reappears, which is the reason for the repetitious couplet at the end of each verse. This poem became a favorite among the inmates who knew Frankie San.

The Navigator

I stood upon a desert isle,
    Amid a sea of desert isles,
As great green waves came rolling in
    And washed back out to sea again.

I saw upon each desert strand
    There stood one lost and lonely man.
As great green waves came rolling in
    And washed back out to sea again.

Upon my isle one stout tree grew,
    Each other isle had one tree too.
I thought, "I'll fell this mighty tree
    And venture out upon the sea."

And so with shells and stones and hand,
    I finally brought my tree to land;
As great green waves came rolling in
    And washed back out to sea again.

As my talk came to an end
    I said, "I'll go and find a friend,
And if it be a friend I find,
    We'll fell his tree; lash it to mine.

And we will travel each wet mile
    Until we've touched at every isle."
As great green waves came rolling in
    And washed back out to sea again.

So at each isle we'll gain a tree
    And gain new friends, my friend and me.
Thus we will build a mighty raft
    As seaworthy as any craft.

We would be lost no more, you see?
    And we could sail the awesome sea.
As great green waves came rolling in
    And washed back out to sea again.

We'd search until we found a land
    Where men gave man a helping hand
And where there were no desert isle
    To cut us off from friendly smiles,

Where all men called the sea a friend
    And not a fence between good men.
As great green waves came rolling in
    And washed back out to sea again.

I launched my log; I climbed astride;
    I fought the waves and wind and tide.
As I drew near the nearest beach
    The man thereon leaped to his feet.

He watched my fight from crest to crest;
    I flailed and beat at Neptune's breast,
As great green waves came rolling in
    And washed back out to sea again.

At last I won through to the man,
    Stepped from the sea, stretched forth my hand.
"Ho, friend," I called. "See that lone tree?
    I've made great plans for it and thee!"

But not a word or sign gave he.
    He cast me back into the sea.
As great green waves came rolling in
    And washed back out to sea again.

He gathered stones, and shells, and more,
    Threw them to drive me from his shore;
I set back out to sea again –
    Set out to find some other friend.

I knew among these shipwrecked men
    There must be more who searched for friends,
As great green waves came rolling in
    And washed back out to sea again.

And so I floated on my log,
    I breasted wind, and tide, and fog.
I landed at each desert isle
    But nowhere found a friendly smile.

My arms grew weak, my spirit low;
    There were but few more miles to go.
As great green waves came rolling in
    And washed back out to sea again.

Some men would not let me land.
    Some waited 'til they heard my plan,
Then turned and cast me back to sea.
    Some tried to take my log from me.

A few said, "Stay, and be my friend,
   But let us not seek other men."
As great green waves came rolling in
   And washed back out to sea again.

Until one day at last I found
   Beneath my feet familiar ground.
Beside a bitter, brackish pool
   I saw a crude shell-cutting tool;

There grew inside my chest a lump
   As I gazed on an old tree stump.
As great green waves came rolling in
   And washed back out to sea again.

I stood upon my desert isle
   Amid a sea of desert isles.
I looked out o'er the restless sea
   At lonely men who looked like me.

And so my log I cast aside;
   I sat upon the sand and cried.
As great green waves came rolling in
   And washed back out to sea again.

And then one day across the sea,
   A man came floating, on a tree.
He called, "Ho, friend, I braved the sea –
   Yon is a stump; where is the tree?

Come let us make some seaweed twine
   And lash your tree fast to mine!"
As great green waves came rolling in
   And washed back out to sea again.

He said, "We'll cross to the next man
    And he will aid us in my plan.
We'll . . ." but no other word spoke he,
    I cast him back into the sea.

I searched around for shell and stone
    And drove him from my desert home.
As great green waves came rolling in
    And washed back out to sea again.

As the stranger pulled away
    I thought of what I'd heard him say.
I thought the words I'd heard before
    Upon some other desert shore.

"But this," I thought, "it cannot be,
    I've been here since eternity."
As great green waves came rolling in
    And washed back out to sea again.

And then one day I looked to see
    A small, small ship far out at sea;
It seemed to leap before the wind
    With bobbing spar, so neat, so trim.

I watched its flight with joyous eye.
    I feared that it might pass me by.
As great green waves came rolling in
    And washed back out to sea again.

It came from where the sun was born
    To march across the sky each morn.
And as the sun it shed a light
    So that I watched it through the night.

Its course was true, it never veered;
 The sea of desert isles it neared.
As great green waves came rolling in
 And washed back out to sea again.

I knew the Captain of this craft
 Could hold his course with ship or raft:
Or even clinging to a tree
 Could navigate the entire sea.

I looked upon my fallen tree
 And thought, "Oh, what a friend he'd be."
As great green waves came rolling in
 And washed back out to sea again.

I watched the small, trim ship for miles
 'Til it touched on a desert isle.
The lonely man it rescued there
 Had named his desert isle "Despair."

And many more such names found he;
 'Twas "Greed," and "Hate," and "Jealousy."
As great green waves came rolling in
 And washed back out to sea again.

So he passed from isle to isle
 'Til he came to my desert isle.
As closer to my isle he came
 On the ship's side I read again,

And kneeling on the island's sand
 I read in gold, "The Frankie San."
As great green waves came rolling in
 And washed back out to sea again.[40]
   – Bob (to Frankie San, 1965)

---

40 Excerpt from *Cell 55*, August 1966.

Such was Bob's insight into the role Frankie played in salvation through Christ. He sailed into the prison with love and returned again and again to touch the hearts of the deserted men.

Often when school was over for the day, Frankie stopped by Bob's living quarters. Bob helped Frankie work on his handicaps – his poor English skills and other cultural things. They sat on the floor and chatted and studied through the bars.

"Bob, where can I find *Christ wept, saying O Jerusalem, Jerusalem* or something? . . . Oh yes, that's right. How about the lost-coin story?"

Then he said, "Let me see, Bob, oh, yes; if she had ten coins and lost one, . . . then *she calls together her friends and neighbors, saying, 'Rejoice with me, for I have found the coin which I had lost!' (Luke 15:9)."*

At the end of an evening of studying and searching Scripture with Bob, Frankie left. He crossed the prison yard, often seeing the moon and stars overhead.

James

James experienced crime and prison for more than thirty-three years. He started in reform school but moved on to prison – nine times – and three times on to old chain gangs. He had been shot five times, stabbed numerous times, and faced violence in and out of prison.

One day Frankie summoned James to the library because he had recognized his efforts to reform and to help others. Frankie saw him care for the animals and gain a trust with them. James told Frankie that he was living proof that criminals can reform – even after thirty years in prison. He wrote about Frankie San:

Frankie was a man who battled darkness and hate for twenty-eight years (at the time this was written) with a sword of love. He appeared to be the most unlikely man to succeed at reaching prisoners and inspiring them to reach up and out of the darkness and horrors of prison. Many prisoners did not trust him or understand him at first because it was hard to hear someone tell them he loved them.

Prisoners and officials often made fun of Frankie San; he regularly met opposition to his endeavors of love. He was cursed, spit on, and threatened, but he continued to care for all, regardless of their crimes or hostile acts toward him. The more despised and damned a prisoner was, the more Frankie San reached out to him. He gave special attention and actions of love to those on Death Row.

Frankie endured the riots and daily violence but pushed forward until all the prisoners knew that he was the best thing that ever happened at CCI.

James said that what Frankie San accomplished in the library was proof that the most hardened criminal could be reached and would respond to acts of extended trust, kindness, care, and love.

Charles

Frankie met Charles in the brickmason yard one morning. His hair stood straight up and his face was red as a beet.

"&#%!@?, #$%&, **!!@+##!"

A little stunned, Frankie replied, "What's happening? Don't get so mad."

"#%@&??>**!"

Charles couldn't say a civil word to Frankie, so Frankie decided he wasn't feeling so well. He said, "I talk to you sometime later."

A few days later Frankie saw him in the yard, so he ran to the commissary and bought a bar of soap for him. Frankie often gave gifts of soap to the men. He trotted back out and handed the soap to Charles.

"What's this? Why do you give me this? Why?" Then he opened his big mouth and burst out laughing – almost like one would imagine Goliath laughing. "I got it. You want me to wash my mouth out with this soap, don't you?" Charles laughed and laughed.

Frankie did not know what to say, but the soap made him laugh, and that was good. That day a bar of soap touched Charles's heart, which cemented their friendship. Later Frankie found out that Charles was one of the roughest guys there, but since that time, he came and talked freely with Frankie. He was another lonely man behind the high, razor-wired walls. He had tried to "do good" but failed time after time. He had no father, and his mother died when he was one. With no one to show him God's love, he became a repeat offender.

When Frankie asked Charles to write something about his life, he briefly wrote of how he went from stealing eggs to armed robbery. Then he continued to explain what a fool he'd been and how he hated himself, but he recognized that there was a power in the prison, not of brute force or supreme power, that could make him into the man he wanted to be. He knew it was the power of brotherly love that radiated from every pore of a tiny body – the body that was fondly called "Frankie San." Charles said that he had at last met a human being who loved his fellow man more than he loved himself.

At thirty-three years old, Charles had done six prison stints. The longest time he had spent outside the walls since the age of fourteen was six months, but in just a few weeks, the little Japanese man had changed his outlook and softened his heart.

A couple weeks after Charles wrote his first piece for Frankie, he showed up with another piece – and a poem. In a couple paragraphs, he wrote of a message that finally reached his heart. The insightful poem he titled "Look."

"Look." Look into my life,
   And there you will see,
What a warped and twisted person
   Sin and corruption can cause one to be.

"Look." Look at all the anguish, misery I have sown,
   By making others bear the burdens that were rightly my own.
But at last I realize now, that they are my own.
   When a person changes, if they really can,
It seems like forgiveness for so much
   Will take more than one life span.

"Look." Look my brothers,
   This message to you I construe,
If not but for the grace of God
   It would not be me
BUT YOU.[41]

Irwin

Irwin was on the work buses that passed Angelo's restaurant when Frankie first took note of the prisoners. In fact, the waving and bowing went on for months, and the prisoners enjoyed this break in their daily monotony.

When Frankie showed up at the prison and asked to meet these worker inmates, Irwin was one of the first to meet him. Frankie asked each one if he could do anything to help them, but since they didn't believe he could work a miracle, they just thanked him and went on their way. Frankie was by far the weakest-looking man they had ever met.

---

41   Excerpts and adaptations from *Cell 55*, September 1966.

Irwin struggled with alcohol and drugs. Though he had studied the philosophy and wisdom of many great men, none of that could help him. No words could describe the pain he experienced from withdrawal. He wondered how the weakling Japanese man could stay straight. Was it really God? Irwin cried out to God, "Almighty God, help me as you have helped others. I have no pride left, no life that is mine, for it belongs to the drug flowing in my veins."

Irwin fell to his knees and asked God to save him from his living hell, and as he kneeled, the pain subsided, and he was no longer afraid. After that, his life gradually changed, for he studied the book of true knowledge, the Bible. Irwin noticed how Frankie gave up all things that other people consider valuable, and became an outcast with them. Frankie, the one that Irwin considered the little Japanese weakling, became the personification of a strength that goes far beyond mortal understanding. He brought to life the words of the apostle Paul: *My grace is sufficient for you, for power [strength] is perfected in weakness* (2 Corinthians 12:9).

Irwin admitted that it was not easy, but his other way of life was intolerable. While physically a prisoner, spiritually he became a free man. Free from doubt, free from anxiety, and free from his living hell. Frankie's radiance, love, and devotion portrayed the love of Christ to Irwin in a way that he could find the peace that all men seek.[42]

Robert

Frankie's work was not easy. He suffered much and experienced great pain as he worked with inmates. Often he did not know if he could make it the following day, but the Lord enabled

---

42 Adapted from an excerpt from *Cell 55*, 1967.

him to face the difficulty and hardship. He moved forward by remembering the reason for his labors.

Frankie first met Robert as he waited to be taken to his cell on death row. Robert's story was the sad one of the abused becoming the abuser and then the criminal. Frankie walked right up to him and started looking through the little candy box he held. Robert was not excited to see a guy with the "collar"; he thought Frankie was a priest.

"What you got in here?" Frankie asked. "Let me have look at what you got in here."

Robert was irritated by the little, nosy Japanese "priest" who talked funny. Frankie looked through everything in the little box and then said, "I bring you what you need. I be right back."

Robert was assigned to cell 8. He sat down; there were no sheets for the mattress or anything else. The guard told him it would be Monday before he could get some. About that time, Frankie returned with his arms loaded down with what looked like half a department store. He brought sheets, pillowcases, shirts, shower shoes, paper, envelopes, towels, and soap. Everything Robert needed.

Then he leaned real close to Robert and slipped him ten dollars. "Watch yourself around these guys; you be careful and keep to yourself." Then just as quickly as he had appeared, he disappeared.

For years, yes, years, Frankie persevered as he tried to talk to Robert, but Robert would not even respond when Frankie delivered books to his cell. He was hostile and suspicious. One time Frankie bought Robert a television set, which Robert proceeded to sell to pay back some money he had borrowed. Frankie usually sent money orders to Robert every month, but for some reason they were not delivered for two months, and Robert had needed money.

Later he felt guilty about selling the television and told Frankie,

"I am sorry. I know you must think bad of me because of this, but I would rather go ahead and tell you the truth about this and hope you understand and don't stop being a friend to me." Frankie would not consider ceasing to be a friend to one of the guys. In fact, when this incident came up much later, Frankie did not even remember it. More than likely, he replaced the television, but the details of the incident escaped him.

Eventually Robert opened up, and Frankie was able to share his own story with him. He told about coming home to a devastated country after the war, defeated and depressed, and he told about trying to commit suicide. About a year later Robert handed Frankie a letter which said, "You really cared about what happened to me. Through you, Frankie San, my brother, I have found Jesus Christ, and I have come to know the true meaning of love. The two most important events in my life will always be the day we met and the night I got down on my knees in my cell and asked Jesus Christ into my life."

That night Frankie went back to his room in the guards' quarters and cried and cried – with great joy. After all those years, one inmate accepted the Lord in his cell. Robert's story was a testimony to the fact that even in the dark shadows of death row, the love of Jesus Christ can enable a long-dormant heart to blossom like a flower in the light of a fresh spring day.

Robert also proved to be a gifted writer. His specialty was haiku, and he often sent the little poems to Frankie. One poem in particular spoke of his conversion:

> From the rising sun
> My brother came harvesting
> The fields of a new land.

> The Death Row man
> On his knees
> Accepting Jesus.

He wrote to Frankie that he now understood the full meaning of trust. He had been afraid to trust Frankie, but Frankie introduced him to Jesus. After that, Robert learned to trust.[43] He put it this way: "My cries echoed all my life the pain I felt – lonely and alone. Then like a father bringing his child a warm glass of milk to enable him to sleep, you, Frankie, brought me the Good News, Jesus Christ. Now my cries are stilled. See what you have done, my brother, from the land of the Rising Sun. This time you don't bomb Pearl Harbor. You bomb my doubt and fears."

When all appeals failed, in spite of a brain tumor that may have affected his behavior, Robert faced his execution. Frankie sat with him in his cell on the eve of that fateful day, and they ate a last supper together – pepperoni pizza. After midnight they walked together to the execution chamber. Robert was peaceful and bade Frankie farewell. He said, "I'm all right, Frankie. Thank you for everything you have done for me."

Later Frankie found a note Robert had left him. It said, "I want to assure you that I'm okay with God, and that I have made my peace with Him. . . . My mind and spirit are with Jesus. See you on the other side one day."[44]

One more time Frankie had lived out Matthew 25:35-36:

> *For I was hungry, and you gave Me something to eat; I was thirsty, and you gave Me something to drink; I was a stranger, and you invited Me in; naked, and you clothed Me; I was sick, and you visited Me; I was in prison, and you came to Me.*

---

43   Adapted from *Cell 55*, Christmas 1987.
44   "Springtime Greetings by Frankie San," Spring 1998.

Mac and Tommy

One day Frankie had played ball with some inmates at the maximum security center. When they were finished, he walked outside the building and stopped at Tommy's cell. Inside were three tiers and a basement area called the "hole." The place had four heavy iron doors and was like a dungeon. Four feet separated the cells from the outside window, so the men were not able to peer outside. Rough guys were sent to this hole.

From outside one broken window Frankie called, "Tommy, are you there?"

"Oh, is that you, Frankie? I'm glad to see you."

"What do you need today, Tommy?"

"Well, I need a few stamps and envelopes so I can write Mother a letter. I can also use a few chips (prison money)."

"Okay, Tommy, I'll get them soon."

Then another voice came from within. "Hey man, I gotta talk to you."

"Who is that, Tommy?"

"Oh, that's Mac; he's in the next cell."

"Okay. Hey man, what you want?" Frankie called down.

"I'm Mac. I just want to talk to someone," he replied.

"It's so dark in there I can't see you. Why can't I go to other side door?" So Frankie went inside the building. "Officer, who is Mac?"

"Mac? Oh, you are in deep trouble, Frankie. You don't want to mess with that guy."

Well, Frankie didn't like that advice. He had been in trouble for ten years; one more trouble did not faze him. He went to the warden's office. "Warden, sir, I want to see Mac in the hole."

"You do? Well, he is a tough character. I haven't been able to reach him yet. In fact, nobody can talk to him. Be my guest, but be careful. Take one of my officers with you."

"Is this necessary?" Frankie asked.

"Yes," he answered firmly.

So Frankie went with the officer down to the basement; he opened the heavy door. There was another barred door and a small hole. Frankie reached out his hand and shook Mac's hand through the hole. Mac was able to carry on an intelligent conversation, and Frankie noticed many books and papers on his bunk. Supposedly, Mac was not able to communicate with others because he was so violent, but Frankie was able to speak with him. Mac's shooting, attacking others, and taking hostages did not affect Frankie, but he puzzled over how to help him.

Mac wrote poems and essays, many about his loneliness. One of Frankie's outside friends sent Mac a gift; another sent his mother a gift. Frankie continued to visit Mac on a regular basis and Mac started to change. As Christmas approached, Mac wrote to the warden to request the opportunity to take a collection from the other men to buy Frankie a plaque. All of the officers were shocked that such kindness should come from Mac.

So they collected whatever they could, and on Christmas Eve when Frankie entered the maximum security gate, he heard joyful music and screaming laughter. He approached Mac's cell and looked inside. Mac wasn't there. Frankie looked under the bunk. Mac wasn't there either. Finally, Frankie said, "Officer, Mac isn't inside the cell."

"Oh, he's out there with the warden."

Frankie turned and saw Mac – out of his hole. Mac approached the microphone and said, "Ya'll be quiet one minute." Every man stood by his cell door and hushed. "Tonight, ya'll know what we try to do for our Santa." Frankie stood beside him. "Frankie, we all appreciate your bringing us cheer and joy each Christmas Eve. This is just a small token of our sincere appreciation." Then Mac presented Frankie with the plaque commemorating his profound humanitarian work.

Frankie was speechless. He knew how little these men had to give, but they had given him this very personal gift. Tears welled up in his eyes and dropped onto the plaque. Frankie declared, "See what fine men they are if we give them opportunities."[45]

Joseph

Joseph was a self-taught artist at CCI when Frankie met him. He was very quiet and they seldom talked, but Frankie loved his paintings. By the time Joseph had finished about a dozen paintings for Frankie, he was transferred to another state prison.

As they corresponded, Joseph's openness about himself surprised Frankie. Their friendship blossomed and they poured their hearts out to each other. They complimented and encouraged one another and even criticized the other's faults.

Frankie learned much about the criminal mind from Joseph. He listened to the meanings behind the words and tried to comprehend such a lifestyle. Frankie wanted to know how he thought and what he believed. Their mutual acceptance aided him in understanding the struggles and desires of a person trapped in a life of crime. Through his letters, Joseph taught Frankie many things.

For example, when Joseph first started doing crime, he thought it was a way to get rich quick. After many years of being in and out of jail, he realized this "getting rich quick" scheme wouldn't work, but it was the only thing he knew how to do. So he continually went back to stealing.

One time when Frankie had made a suggestion to Joseph, Joseph admitted that Frankie was having an influence on him. He said it was very hard for him to act like a hard-core convict

---

45   Adapted from "On Christmas Eve," by Frankie San, *Cell 55*, January 1977.

when Frankie kept telling him to do something worthwhile with the rest of his life. As he thought about that, he realized he wanted to be remembered for something. He had accepted that the Lord loved him, cared for him, knew his turmoil better than anyone, and knew why he was the way he was. Joseph knew God was aware that he was not able to change himself – or even have the desire to change.

Joseph had no family or home to turn to when he was released, but comments in his letters made it clear that Frankie encouraged him to move to Columbia, South Carolina, and work with him. Frankie even referred to him as his brother – and sometimes as his son. Joseph said he'd be a dog as long as he could be part of Frankie's family. Joseph in turn encouraged Frankie when Frankie admitted he was discouraged and suffering.

Later, Joseph admitted that most of the inmates could change, but they needed a reason and an example. He told Frankie that in his quiet way of listening and offering help, he did more than all of the other preachers. Joseph knew Frankie put all of his trust in God but said he and the other inmates were godless or they wouldn't be in prison. He said most did not even know how to trust, and along with distrust came the inability to love.

Frankie continually reassured Joseph that he was a "good guy" and "capable of being honest." After many, many letters, Joseph said Frankie had inspired him. He said he believed in God, but he still had some misconceptions about Him.

Frankie's work with Joseph was slow and continual. He had learned that when these men had spent most of their lives in crime of one kind or another, the process of changing the heart was usually slow. But change they could.[46]

---

46   Adapted from *Cell 55*, Christmas 1983.

Randy

Sometimes when a family member ends up in prison, the rest of the family is able to continue in their own spiritual growth. They still care for the one in prison and write letters of encouragement. Randy was one such blessed prisoner. He had run wild and done drugs for so long that he didn't care about anyone but himself. When he was finally locked up, he was glad, because he was hurting and knew he was causing his parents a lot of trouble.

But Randy declared that even though he was in prison, that particular year was the most rewarding time spiritually that he'd ever experienced. His parents wrote to him about a new preacher who was young, active, and desired to get involved with helping people. This surprised Randy because he could not ever remember his parents being that excited about a preacher. After Randy's mom told the preacher about Randy and his work in the library with Frankie, he wrote to Frankie and invited him to the church for the weekend after Thanksgiving. Even though that time of year was always busy for Frankie, it just happened that he didn't have plans for that weekend. So he went.

Randy's parents had come to visit on the Saturday after Thanksgiving, so Frankie was able to follow them home all the way to North Carolina. Poor Randy sat in prison all weekend wondering how it was going. To his delight, the preacher's wife made a video of their time with Frankie, so he could take it back to the prison and show Randy.

Frankie shared his story with the church and told them how he came to America to start a new life. He told them how hard it was with the language and lessons. Then he told them about an inmate who was an artist and who gave him some of his paintings. Then he showed them what Christmas and Easter were like in prison by dressing up like Santa and the Easter bunny. The whole congregation laughed and cried tears of joy.

The real joy was Randy's, however, and he hugged Frankie and cried his own tears of joy. It made him happy to see the love that the people had for him. He was thankful that his parents welcomed Frankie and said it seemed as though through Frankie, part of him was with the congregation, laughing and feeling warm.

Frankie explained to Randy that through the Holy Spirit, they could touch each other's souls. Through the Spirit, believers can share so deeply that there is a bonding and a kinship that only happens after they have found God. Randy's parents were able to see this in Randy, and seeing their happiness brought joy to Randy.

Randy credited Frankie for helping to change his life. Frankie even convinced Randy that he could do something to help other prisoners' lives. He helped Randy see the love of his parents. Randy declared that Frankie would always be part of his family because he owed his life to him. He said, "If I would die in prison today, I would have no regrets of my past, because God has forgiven me, and I have a true friend for life."

Caring for the families of the prisoners was just one more way that Frankie lived Christ before these people. Christ loves all of them, so Frankie loved all of them and showed that love any way he could – even driving to North Carolina on Thanksgiving weekend.

> *For God so loved the world, that He gave His only begotten Son, that whoever believes in Him shall not perish, but have eternal life. For God did not send the Son into the world to judge the world, but that the world might be saved through Him.* (John 3:16-17)[47]

---

47   Adapted from *New Year's Newsletter*, February 1989.

Randy's story did not end there. In fact, that was just the beginning. When his parole hearing came up, Frankie joined his parents and Pastor Cash to stand beside Randy that day. The chances for anyone from CCI to make parole the first time they met the board were slim to none. Family and friends back home held a prayer vigil for Randy, and even Frankie admitted to selfishly asking God for Randy's parole.

When Randy's number was called for him to go in, his knees and hands shook, and he was scared to death; they all went in. Seven serious parole members stared at Randy. The stern-looking one asked Randy a couple questions. Then he gave Randy's mother an opportunity to say a few words. He didn't ask any other questions. They were not asked to leave the room, but instead, the board announced that Randy was paroled.

A week later Randy wrote to Frankie and reported that he was doing great. He had a job and spent time helping his mother and dad. He mowed the lawn and helped in the garden. He commented on how good the dirt smelled and that he enjoyed driving the tractor. One night he cooked supper and washed the dishes. Mostly, he told Frankie that he loved him and appreciated what he had done for him. Randy said, "If it wasn't for you, I'd still be in bed number fourteen."

Frankie visited the home of Randy's family several months later to see how he was doing. They sat at a picnic table in the backyard and enjoyed the peacefulness of the countryside together. Sitting silently, they were both caught up in that special moment.[48] The words of a famous hymn came to Frankie's mind:

> This is my Father's world,
> And to my listening ears
> All nature sings, and round me rings
> The music of the spheres.

---

48 Adapted from *Cell 55*, Christmas 1990.

This is my Father's world:
I rest me in the thought
Of rocks and trees, of skies and seas—
His hand the wonders wrought.[49]

The green, green, green grass of Randy's home blessed the prodigal son who had returned. Frankie and Randy both thanked God for that moment.

Thomas

Most of the work that Frankie did with the men was a labor of patience and love. He did not appear one day and change everybody's life. Far from it. The transforming of a criminal is not an overnight event, so Frankie trudged on with one act of love after another.

Thomas noticed that Frankie was always around and seemed to care for everyone. One time he brought Thomas a "new glass" – a mirror. The label said it was unbreakable, so Thomas took it, turned it upside down on the floor, and stood on it. It didn't break. Well, that didn't suit him, so he placed it on its side and stood on it that way. It shattered. Like a little boy, he stared at Frankie and said, "Someone lied."

Then Thomas offered to pay for it, but Frankie would not consider that. What's more – the incident was never mentioned again. Thomas watched Frankie buy many items for the inmates – clothes, shoes, and even TVs. When Thomas realized that one of the guys had sold his TV to buy dope, he told Frankie, expecting him to hit the roof. All he did was put his hand on Thomas's shoulder and say, "It's awright, Big Tom. When I give it to him, it is his to do what he wants with it."

49   Maltbie D. Babcock, "This is My Father's World," 1901, *www.hymnary.org/text/this_is_my_fathers_world_and_to_my*

When Thomas found out that another guy had spit in Frankie's face, he wanted to know who it was. He asked over and over, but Frankie wouldn't tell. He just said, "It's okay. I will not tell you."

Many times when they heard fights starting, Thomas saw Frankie walk down to the middle of it. He'd put out his hands and call the prisoners by name. He'd end the whole thing by asking, "What would your mother say?" or "You will not be able to see your children. Stop it! Give me that knife." Risky? Yes, but Frankie was able to do it.

After watching Frankie call everyone by name and working with him in the library, Thomas knew that he needed Frankie's help. He was the broken glass that needed repair, and Frankie was the patient, soft-spoken face of Christ who offered the repair manual. Thomas's life changed little by little, and today he says, "No mere words can show you who Frankie was or is to us." His love was always evident.

Another inmate wrote, "I have the hope that my children will forgive me, because a man I once hated has forgiven me; and this Father's Day I will honor him. By his actions, he has compelled my respect, and by his forgiveness, he gained my love. In a transplanted Japanese preacher, I found a father figure. . . . He has shown me the face of Christ."

Jimmy

Like so many others, Jimmy came from a broken home and held down a job at fourteen to support himself. His father had taught him to be independent, but he also liked having his own money. However, by working late nights Jimmy hung out with an older bunch and had access to drugs and alcohol.

Jimmy was sentenced to three years after being convicted of heroin possession, but those three years turned out to be a school for crime – how to steal like professionals and how to deal drugs in a business fashion. When he returned to the streets, he was like a wild animal that had escaped its cage. He was angry and hurting but couldn't talk to anyone. Before long he had killed two men; he was sentenced to die in the electric chair.

Because the appeals process was so slow, Jimmy spent eighteen years under the death sentence – eleven of which were in solitary confinement, a prison within a prison. During this time he penned an essay entitled "Lonely Days, Lonely Knights," which not only described the helpless and hopeless state of the incarcerated soul, but also illustrated the skill Jimmy possessed with words. In a portion of that essay, he said:

> The armor-suited warrior walks resolutely towards his destination: the end of another day. Wasted time. Lost dreams. His suit shines in the glow of dusk, as do the bars, the fences, and the barbed wire that surround him. And therein lies the cruel irony – that as the bars and fences keep him in, so the cold, hard armor of his suit keeps others out.
>
> If chivalry is dead, someone forgot to tell the knights of lonely days, the faceless entities among thousands of masked warriors that stroll the halls of the house of the dead. It's the arena of slow death – prison in America.
>
> The gallant knights stride each day toward the months – and years. Time is their nemesis, acknowledging its passing their only solace. They continue to fearlessly fight on, striving from battle to battle, until at last they must stop to ask what war they are fighting. Many others, lost and forgotten, struggle to maintain hope and sanity, spirit

and dignity. Some lose the war, succumbing to faded hope, faded dreams, faded life.

The war of attrition wages on. Tired soldiers trudge forward, not in camaraderie but each alone in his struggle. Watchful adversaries in uniform stand guard like sentries, observing and scrutinizing all. There is no privacy. There is no peace. Caustic commands from authoritarian voices blare constantly. Their tone is unrelentingly harsh in tempo. But the armored warrior shows no emotion, just the steely countenance of one determined to arrive at his destination.

Only the closest of confidants ever glimpse the real person within. He mustn't divulge the pain he feels, the loneliness or boredom that throbs in his bones like the acne of a cancer. To reveal the pain, to allow others to witness his "weakness" is to become prey to the unmerciful, unrelenting torture from others seeking to vent their own misery and blighted lives. For them, inflicting pain acts as an anesthetic for their own travails.

The armored knight strides determinedly towards his destination, never wavering, never looking back, for the demon may be gaining. He strives for his freedom, the place where he thinks he can finally shed his protective armor. Then at last he can emerge whole. But he still has battles to fight, wars to win. Not until he has opened his heart and once again begun to trust his fellow man can he be absolutely free. So many lonely days. Too many lonely knights.[50]

---

50   Excerpt from "Lonely Days, Lonely Knights," by Jimmy, July 1995.

Jimmy's essay portrayed the life of a human living in an inhuman manner, in a prison of his own making. This was the challenge that Frankie faced, but, like he did with so many others, he visited Jimmy on death row and brought him soap, books, and words of encouragement. In time, Jimmy's death sentence was commuted to a life sentence due to changes in South Carolina law.

Frankie told Jimmy that he cared and offered him a job in the library. At first, Jimmy could not relate to what Frankie taught, but he watched, listened, and helped when he could. He learned to reach out to others and to care for them; he then became a counselor and assisted others with their problems. He found out that by helping the guys, he helped himself. All through this, Jimmy became closer to Frankie and realized that the spiritual, emotional, and moral foundation he was gaining was the greatest feeling he ever had. He attributed his growth to the Lord and Frankie.

Eventually, Frankie's love broke through that hardened exterior, and the battle-scarred, grayed knight became a devout follower of Jesus Christ, and through His healing Spirit found purpose, fulfillment, and that oh-so-elusive gift of peace. "Lonely Days, Lonely Knights" became "Christ-Filled Days, Peace-Filled Knights." Jimmy's growth opened the door for him to reside in a Character-Based Unit, a pilot program designed to integrate faith and opportunity among a select group of inmates. He spent his days as a teacher, mentor, and supportive friend to others as he realized that his gift of teaching was a blessing to both himself and to those with whom he could share his hard-earned life lessons.

As a man of peace, he could now wear the glorious armor of God – the belt of truth, the breastplate of righteousness, feet shod with the gospel of peace, the shield of faith, the helmet of salvation, and the sword of the Spirit. In his own words, Jimmy said:

> The armor of God shines more brightly each day with the understanding that as one of God's warriors, the battle is won – not with brute force but with character. Always polished, the armor is ready and prepared for the spiritual battle that must be fought with God's strength, for the human effort is inadequate, but God's power is invincible. The peace-filled knight battles on, seeking his strength, courage, and guidance in the Holy Spirit and the gospel, for which he lives as "an ambassador in chains" and wherever in His grace He leads me.
>
> This old soul, in chains almost four decades, can now finally embrace that once so elusive, calming, and glorious peace. . . . To shed the cold, human shell that hinders life and adopt the enduring, edifying, loving warmth of Jesus Christ is to find peace and freedom no matter your station in this glorious, eternal journey.
>
> So many Christ-filled days, never enough peace-filled knights.

Through Frankie's long, patient love and ministry, Jimmy was transformed, and his heart had softened such that he could love and serve the Lord. Jimmy said, "Frankie, you are a special man in every way. Please remember, you have been my teacher and mentor. By watching you help and guide others, I too have learned that helping others is what life is all about. I never wanted to die not caring about anyone, and I have genuine love in my heart for everyone."

Later Jimmy wrote, "For almost four decades I've witnessed your example, and only now, on the eve of my fifty-seventh birthday, do I feel the full impact of His message. 'Let love be your greatest aim.' Love is the means by which spiritual gifts are made effective."

In response to some of the praise he received, Frankie said, "This is what I've done all these years. I just loved these men, but do not forget that this is God's story, not mine. He gave me this great opportunity and I took it."[51]

> *Therefore in Christ Jesus I have found reason for*
> *boasting in things pertaining to God. For I will*
> *not presume to speak of anything except what*
> *Christ has accomplished through me, resulting in*
> *the obedience of the Gentiles by word and deed.*
> (Romans 15:17-18)

---

51   Excerpt from *Cell 55*, Summer 2005.

Chapter 12

Triumph, Tragedy, and Sadness

Pat

Often triumph occurs in the midst of tragedy. That was the case when a death row inmate was killed in a bombing as the result of a "contract murder." It was paid for by someone outside the prison system. Fighting and killing were not uncommon, but contract murders were. When the public heard of this, they started an investigation that turned the prison upside down to discover the reason.

In the midst of this, however, an inmate went to Frankie and admitted that he had hated him for five years. He hated him because he was a preacher, because he was a "Jap," and because he seemed to favor others. Pat needed someone to hate, and he "gave Frankie the full load." He had first come to Frankie in 1978 to ask for money for college. Frankie gave it to him but didn't see him again until 1983.

Pat had confessed to a crime he did not commit to save his wife and the wife of a friend from prison. He had escaped from prison and was free for two years, but he was recaptured and returned to prison. Once again Pat's world had fallen apart, and he was broken, bitter, and desperate. Out of desperation, he went without hope and expected tricks, but he asked Frankie for advice. Pat had only known bitterness and hatred as a child, and disappointment and failure as an adult. Pat had never known his father, though he wanted that relationship. Ironically, he fathered eleven children but raised none of them. He knew they suffered because of him, but he forfeited his right to their respect and love.

When he was recaptured, it was not because he broke any law but because he had tried to bring his family together. Pat's son, whom he had not seen in twenty years, assisted in his recapture. Pat's heart pumped hatred through his body, and his mind was drugged with that hate, but he later realized that God put him back in prison. His salvation waited for him. He was a bitter, godless man, but the very hate was what God used to show him love.

Pat had spent Father's Day in taverns, hotel rooms, and prison – wishing he could change things. This day always brought remorse and regret. He did not fault anyone but himself, but he had discovered there was forgiveness in this world; he only hoped that someday his children would forgive him too.

Pat said he had that hope because of Frankie – a man he had once hated who forgave him. On one particular Father's Day, he said, "I will honor him (Frankie). By his actions, he has compelled my respect, and by his forgiveness, he gained my love. In a transplanted Japanese preacher, about my age, I found a father figure."

Within a week of opening up to Frankie, a transformation began. Within a month, he uttered those words that are so hard for convicts: "I love you, Frankie." It was God loving Pat through Frankie that made the difference. Frankie soon discovered Pat's ability to write, which became a great asset in

his spiritual growth and renewed his hope for the future. Out
of the suffering and struggle of Pat's life, God molded a mind
with the ability to help others.[52]

In His Image

As wind and water, soil and air,
    are things that God has wrought;
Is it not He who made the mind
    in which these words are thought?

To tell the story of His Son,
    and tell the tale in rhyme
Is not something I could do
    without God in my mind.

They bore Him up, nailed to the cross,
    and there He hung and died.
The Son of God, His most Beloved,
    for man was crucified.

And even as He hung in pain,
    another was forgiven.
These words He spoke unto the thief,
    "Today we'll be in heaven."

His earthly life was lived so pure,
    man could not make correction.
Perfect was this Son of God,
    from birth to resurrection.

And even now His perfectness
    has not been marred by time.
For He seeks to save a sinner's soul,

---

52   Adapted from *Cell 55*, Christmas 1983.

the one who writes this rhyme.

Yes, wind and water, soil and air
    are things that God has wrought,
but nothing shows His Greatness more,
    than a mind that seeks a thought.[53]
      – Pat (August 30, 1983)

Even though Pat was able to pen such truths in poetry, he continued to fall into depths of despair. He could not tell right from wrong except through punishment. Pat's despair hit Frankie over the head like a sledgehammer beating his greatest hopes into the ground. He wanted to sit and share the truth of Christ with him: *It is a trustworthy statement, deserving full acceptance, that Christ Jesus came into the world to save sinners* (1 Timothy 1:15).

Then Pat would write a poem, and Frankie's own faith in him would be renewed. The last stanzas of "The Journey" are:

Then prison gates once more slammed,
    And there I was alone and damned,
With bitter hate, my mind was crammed,
    The end of my path, this be.

Then a man stepped out and blocked my way,
    He said there comes a better day,
Hear the words I have to say,
    Leave the path you trod.

The words of Christ, spoke this man,
    This little preacher from Japan,
He took me gently by the hand,
    To show me the path to God.

---

53   "In His Image," by Pat, *Cell 55*, Christmas 1983.

> Now we two walk as one,
>   My spiritual childhood has just begun,
>   God has forgiven the things I've done,
>   My pathway is made straight.
>
> This man from "The Land of the Rising Sun,"
>   Has shown me the way to "The Risen Son."
>   And I know that when all is done,
>   We'll meet at Heaven's gate.[54]
>   – Pat

However, Pat's life was on a roller coaster. A few months later he wrote to Frankie and told him he wanted to quit his job in the library where Frankie paid him "scholarship" money to write for the newsletters. Frankie realized he could not live Pat's life for him or handcuff him and force him to look for God's help. So he prayed and wept, and prayed and wept, and prayed some more. Then Frankie heard that Pat had been placed in "lockup," where prisoners are either being punished or waiting for the staff to conduct an investigation.

After two months in lockup, Pat got a pass to go to the library. Frankie welcomed him back as though nothing had happened and eventually gave Pat his job back.

Soon after Pat got out of lockup, he had the opportunity to be a real friend to Frankie. He knew that one of Frankie's dear friends, J.C., was to be executed that day, so he wrote to Frankie. He assured him that he understood the suffering that Frankie was experiencing – that he was living through the execution of a friend and feeling the cold hardness of "the chair." Pat understood that Frankie would lose a part of himself but reassured him that he had done everything possible. He had given freely of his love and assistance to this very shy

---

54 "The Journey," by Pat, *Cell 55*, Christmas 1983.

person for seven years. But Frankie did not get the letter until after the execution.

The previous evening Frankie had prayed and shared communion with J.C. He drew on Christ's well of faith for all the love and compassion, but even that did not seem enough. He wondered why J.C. had to die that way. His heart burst with sorrow as he prepared J.C. for the last hour and asked him if he had any words for his friends on death row. He said, "Tell them to keep fighting, don't give up, and take life more seriously. Don't waste time, and most important, tell them to accept Jesus Christ."

At that moment, a peace came over Frankie. He sensed the Lord telling him that J.C. was His son too and that he would be lifted to heaven. At 10:10 p.m. on January 10, Frankie hugged J.C. for the last time; there were no tears of parting, for the peace and joy of knowing Christ filled both men. As he left the death house, a cold drizzle fell, but Frankie felt neither the cold nor the wetness. He said, "My whole body was overwhelmed by a strange sensation that lifted me above the pain and worry of this world. As I walked toward my house, I realized that eleven people had been sitting with J.C. during the final hours of his life . . . but there had been twelve chairs in that cell where we waited. Then I saw that twelve had waited; Jesus sat on the twelfth chair. Walking through the dark night, His light filled me and I recalled Matthew 18:20: *For where two or three have gathered together in My name, I am there in their midst.*"

A couple hours after the execution, Frankie walked into the library where Pat and his other workers had already gathered. Pat handed him the letter he had written the night before. Pat could have felt neglected or jealous for the time Frankie had spent with J.C. The "old" Pat would have, but the "new" Pat gave him a letter that spoke of understanding and shared his sorrow. Frankie's pupil cared enough to comfort him and reassure him that he did not fail with J.C. The letter lifted his spirits and he was renewed in his faith also – and in his continuing mission with Pat.

A few years later, Pat wrote this about Frankie:

> I was down so low that the bottom looked like up when I first went to Frankie for help. . . . Most people would not have given me a second glance or listened to me . . . but Frankie reached out to me and said, "Take my hand and I will pull you up from where you are. I will let you stand on my shoulders so you can see things you have never seen before." And he did just that.
>
> There are no words to tell how hard it was for Frankie to pull me up. The love and the pain and hardships go beyond words. For seven long years, Frankie fought the demon inside me; at no time was it easy, but he held on and fought on and finally managed to free me. Frankie stood me on his shoulders . . . and let me see the world that God created through His Son, Jesus Christ.
>
> And that is where I now stand: Solid on the Word of Jesus . . . and looking forward to working with Frankie in any way the Lord directs him to use me.
>
> First Thessalonians 5:18 says, *In everything give thanks; for this is God's will for you in Christ Jesus.* So I gave thanks for all the years I spent in prison, for all the hardship and pain I have suffered because I sinned against God, for I now know that this was His will concerning me. Just as I know that it was He who brought me to the prison where

Frankie was waiting, I give thanks for the truth
Frankie made me see: *And you will know the truth,
and the truth will make you free* (John 8:32).

Without Frankie, I would be nothing; but because
of him, I am a whole man with my mind on the
future and my soul in the keeping of Jesus Christ,
my Lord. I love Frankie for many reasons, but
mostly for giving me Jesus.[55]

After Pat was paroled, Frankie helped him get settled as a father
would help a son. One day Pat came home with a car – excitement all over his face. He jumped out of that old car and ran
in and out of the house like a child at Christmas. Frankie had
to leave for a while, but Pat promised him a ride when he got
home. However, when Frankie returned, the car was gone, and
Pat was nowhere to be found. Frankie's feelings were intense
and painful. He waited. No Pat. He listened all night for the
sound of the old car. Silence. He prayed for the front door to
open. Nothing.

By morning, Frankie felt the same terrible desperation that
parents feel when their child has run away. Frankie never saw
him again. One day nearly two decades later, Pat's daughter
called Frankie and told him Pat had died. She said, "I never
knew him apart from the stories in *Cell 55*. Would you please
tell me what you know about him?"

At last Frankie had some closure regarding Pat. He was
unique and their relationship was unique, but the universal
example of what perseverance in faith can do when applied to
our individual relationships with others is not unique.[56]

From the thoughts and words of friends, even friends who

---

55   Adapted from *New Year's Newsletter*, February 1989.
56   Adapted from *Cell 55*, Summer 2007.

are felons, Frankie's character and love shine through. God used an insecure Japanese "tentmaker" to reach the hearts of hardened criminals like Pat.

Tom

Tom also exhibited an affection for the little Japanese man that so many of the guys spoke about. He attributed the endearment the prisoners felt for Frankie to his "bubbling personality, quiet encouragement, sympathetic ear, low-key spiritual advice, and unending kindness." Tom recognized that Japanese culture made it more difficult for a man to leave his home, family, and friends to come to a foreign land to serve God with his life. But Frankie had done just that.

Tom knew that Frankie suffered significant abuse from the inmates. He had been lied to, stolen from, belittled and laughed at, tricked and disappointed. Tom expressed his admiration and respect for how Frankie handled himself and his regret and sorrow for the crimes he had committed. Tom spoke of following Jesus as one who knew Him personally.

Tom worked in the library with Frankie, but after a year, he was bored and wanted to take a different job. However, he got into trouble and was sent to the security building and then to a different institution. One day he took a couple hostages at gunpoint; after twelve hours, he released them, then pointed the gun at himself and took his own life.

Frankie heard about this on the radio, but only later found out it was Tom. Sadness once again flooded into Frankie's world.

Ben and Tim

Frankie met Ben and Tim, two drug-addicted men, in the infirmary in 1998 and struck up a friendship with them. Tim was forty-one years old and had been in and out of prison for twenty years. Ben was thirty-one years old and had been in trouble because of drugs for fifteen years. They both came from comfortable, middle-class backgrounds with loving parents who suffered and struggled right along with them as their addictions ruined their lives.

Burdened for their parents, Frankie wanted to do something special for them. He suggested getting a Valentine card for them in which these men could write a special message to the ones who gave them life and sacrificially raised them. They agreed.

Frankie returned with the cards, and after they wrote the messages of love, he mailed them with a box of Valentine candy. Soon after, these two men were transferred, so it was a while before Frankie learned of the results.

Ben wrote to him and thanked him for his friendship and spiritual guidance. Ben's mother also wrote to Frankie. She thanked him for befriending their son and sending the card, candy, and book *Chicken Soup for the Mother's Soul*. Most importantly, she said, "I still haven't given up on Ben. There's always a prayer on my lips that he will change. . . . I pray that God will take his addiction away from him – not for us, but for himself and his two beautiful children . . . I pray that God will give him strength to do what he has to do." What a blessed response! Truly, God is the God of second chances – and third, and fourth.

The response from Tim was not so uplifting. Tim wrote to Frankie to tell him he got a "really bad letter" from his dad. Tim had hoped that he had begun to repair the damage to the relationship with his parents, but that was not the case. His dad was not able to move on from the bitterness of being used by Tim. He admitted to going for professional help and getting guidance and support to end his relationship with Tim. Hardest of all, he said, "I am telling you not to come to our house when you are released. I am getting a restraining order against you and will call the police if you show up at my door."

In its own tragic way, this response portrays how terrible a price drug addiction can exact by severing the bond between parent and child. Heartbroken, Tim recognized that when he was released later that year, he would be homeless in the dead of winter. That was not a happy, encouraging thought for him, but it happens more than the public realizes.[57]

The stories of Ben and Tim illustrate the work of Frankie San. He loved these men with a godly love, and that love extended to their families. He worked to build bridges and make repairs in relationships, but most of all he wanted to give them hope, *knowing that tribulation brings about perseverance; and perseverance, proven character; and proven character, hope; and hope does not disappoint, because the love of God has been poured out within our hearts through the Holy Spirit who was given to us* (Romans 5:3-5).

Drew

Throughout his decades of service, Frankie gave more than love, honor, and compassion. He helped these men find hope.

Drew had this to say: "I've overloaded you with my problems and still they cannot compare to the things you've seen and experienced. I can close my eyes and picture you standing on the deck of a giant Japanese warship, the sounds of bombs, men yelling, and the noise of the engines in the background, as you look up for the answers to the things that are in your heart. Now your search has ended in a land far away from your homeland. And because of you, mine is just beginning."

Drew wrote a story, "The Angel Man," in which he captured the essence of Frankie's ministry as he acknowledged how

---

57 "Springtime Greetings from Frankie San," Spring 1998.

Frankie's love for him had engulfed Drew's entire family. He said, "Somehow that love sparked a new relationship between me and my father, Captain Ben, a hard man to get close to."

Frankie had gone to visit Drew's family and walked up to Captain Ben and hugged him. Then he said, "Your son Drew loves you, Captain Ben; I love you too." Drew was shocked when he heard about that because nobody hugged Captain Ben. After the visit, however, Captain Ben wrote to Drew – for the first time ever – and told him that Frankie could visit them anytime he wanted. Drew was so touched he broke down, and tears poured down his cheeks. God's love spilled over from Frankie like a waterfall and generated hope for both inmate and his family.

Drew said, "During my darkest hours when I felt as if all hope was lost, a letter from Frankie would arrive admonishing me and encouraging me to keep up the good fight. He reminded me that with God, hope is never lost."

Chapter 13

Citizenship

One year, early in Frankie's ministry, an inmate asked him what he wanted for Christmas. After some thought, he replied that he wanted to be a citizen of this great country. He loved the United States of America and was grateful to God for calling him here. In his efforts to become an American citizen, he purposely spoke only English, putting aside his native Japanese tongue. He behaved "in Rome as the Romans do." He also set aside the typical reserved manner of the Japanese culture and became outgoing and somewhat aggressive but never self-seeking or self-promoting.

Frankie was not completely Americanized, though, for what sane person would choose to make his home in prison and dedicate his life to those considered the scum of the earth? By man's standards, doing this was weird, strange, and unreal, but Frankie was different. He was committed to Christ and His work.

In spite of all his efforts, Frankie's citizenship did not happen quickly. Maybe he was afraid he would fail because he kept saying, "Wait until next year."

His closest friends came to him one year and said, "This is next year." So Frankie filled out the papers and set things in motion. His friends had to encourage him every day because he was so nervous. They chose several people who knew Frankie well for character witnesses, and the investigator conducted the background study. The investigation went all the way to the midland area of the country, where people told about the little Japanese man with the biggest heart of anyone they knew. They told of his generosity and his love. In the end, the investigator told them that Frankie was the best candidate for citizenship he had ever investigated.

Frankie still had to answer questions and that part worried him most of all. He memorized the presidents' names and some of the South Carolina governors, but when asked about them, his mind went blank. He mumbled an unintelligible something. Then the examiner asked Frankie what he had been doing for twenty years. Well, now Frankie could just talk. He told him the real story in his heart. He explained how God had called him to serve among the criminals. He named every death row inmate, described the riots and fights, and told him about the fun at Christmas and Easter. Frankie then told the examiner how these tough men were his friends, and he had devoted his life to the prison work even though he was not a citizen.

The examiner was bewildered by such a strange applicant and shook his head in amazement. He forgot to ask any more questions. He shook Frankie's hand and said, "That is all, Mr. Frankie San. Good luck to you for your citizenship."

Frankie's friends had waited outside for him – just as nervous as Frankie was. Frankie smiled and everything was all right. He passed with flying colors. The examiner commented that he wished half of the natural citizens cared as much about our nation as Frankie San did. The process was over except for the swearing in.

He was scheduled to appear before U.S. District Court Judge Matthew Perry to be sworn in with others who were becoming citizens. The courtroom was packed with people who wanted to witness their friend Frankie San become a U.S. citizen. The presence of television cameras surprised Judge Perry, but he said nothing about the news coverage. But when the name *Kyuzo Miyaishi* (Frankie San) was read, the cameras began to roll.

Judge Perry remarked, "Now I understand why the television folks are here today." He was not unhappy about the excitement, for he had heard about the unusual little Japanese man who worked with prisoners at the South Carolina Department of Corrections.

After the swearing in, the mayor of Greenville spoke to the group. Tears filled Frankie's eyes and spilled down his cheeks. The group moved to a nearby hotel to celebrate the day.[58]

After twenty years of American life with fourteen of those years serving in the penitentiary, Frankie was granted citizenship. He was fifty-one at the time of his swearing in with fifty-nine other immigrants at the United States District Courthouse. He likened his citizenship to the theme of President Reagan's inauguration theme: "America – A New Beginning."

Frankie said his citizenship was his "marriage" following a long courtship with the United States. "It is the final, total commitment I make to this wonderful country that has given me the opportunity to do the work I do. . . . It is real, real special to me. God found me to do something when He, through this country, gave me this prison and opened its doors to me."[59]

---

58   Adapted from "Tokyo American," *Cell 55*, Christmas 1991.
59   Adapted from *Cell 55*, 1981.

Chapter 14

Beyond the Prison Walls

Raising Funds

Early in his teaching career at CCI, enrollment in Frankie's classes grew, which caused another problem. His limited finances were exhausted. With no other options, he took his crusade beyond the walls. Hat in hand, he went begging. To those who would listen, he challenged them to care, to open their eyes and hearts to the needs of their "caged brothers."

Some people sneered, some openly insulted him, and a trickle responded. The first time a woman sent facecloths and towels, Frankie rushed to the cellblock with a huge smile and tears streaming down his face. "See how people care?" Over and over he repeated those words, and the men were not unaffected.

One prisoner's thank-you note spoke for all of them: "It means a whole lot. It especially hurts deeply having no one at Christmas when you have feelings about what is going on in the free world outside. I have seen how much it hurts even though some men try to hide it; you just can't hold it inside. So you have done a whole lot more than you will ever know, and Christmas will not be just another day here."[60]

---

60   Adapted from an excerpt from "Strange One – This Frankie San," *Cell 55*, 1970.

Other Travels

Though Frankie San spent most of his time in the prison – eating, sleeping, teaching, and ministering within the walls – some weekends and holidays offered him the opportunity to travel to other cities to describe his ministry, request donations, and share the good news of salvation in Jesus Christ. One year right after Christmas he had the privilege of speaking at a regional youth conference in Atlantic City, New Jersey. He chose to speak boldly in his Japanese accent:

> "Yes, there is crisis in Christ's corps because today
> we don't speak up His good news . . . Young men
> and young ladies – BE AMBITIOUS FOR JESUS
> CHRIST!"

In his anxiety and emotion, Frankie was sweating and had to "swallow his breath." Then the light went dim and the auditorium became completely dark. In that blackness, Frankie lit a candle in his hand – a light, a symbol of God in the dark world. With complete silence and no movement in the crowd, he proceeded to sing "Silent Night" in Japanese. Tears streamed down his cheeks.

Frankie recalled, "I finished my witness of His joyful news and bowed. Waiting no time, the audience stood up and clapped their hands excitingly. The joyful clapping sound filled the auditorium, and I bowed again and again."

> *Let the sea roar and all it contains, the world and*
> *those who dwell in it. Let the rivers clap their hands,*
> *let the mountains sing together for joy before the*
> *LORD.* (Psalm 98:7-9)

With almost nineteen hundred youth present, Frankie's joy overflowed. He received many letters from some of them, which extended that joy over a prolonged period of time – particularly the letters indicating that the writers found a new meaning in their lives and realized that God had a purpose for them also.

Frankie exclaimed, "I never dreamed that when I first arrived in America and went to orchards to pick peaches to earn money for my journey to Columbia, South Carolina, that God would take me to magnificent Atlantic City to speak His message."[61]

> *When I came to you, brethren, I did not come with*
> *superiority of speech or of wisdom, proclaiming to*
> *you the testimony of God. For I determined to know*
> *nothing among you except Jesus Christ, and Him*
> *crucified. I was with you in weakness and in fear*
> *and in much trembling, and my message and my*
> *preaching were not in persuasive words of wisdom,*
> *but in demonstration of the Spirit and of power,*
> *so that your faith would not rest on the wisdom of*
> *men, but on the power of God. (1 Corinthians 2:1-5)*

To Bethlehem

Imagine flying above the clouds in a beautiful jetliner, bound for the Holy Land. The excitement and thrill of such a trip would normally encompass all of one's thoughts. But David Barnhart sat next to Frankie San. Though they had been friends for more than a decade, this was the first time David had been able to convince Frankie to leave his "boys" and come away. In fact, it took him five years to get him to leave the prison.

What's more, as David tried to impress upon Frankie what

---

61   Adapted from *Cell 55*, March 1967.

wondrous experiences awaited them, Frankie's heart was still back at the South Carolina state prison. Because it was the day after Easter, Frankie was still full of joy from playing the role of the Easter bunny when he distributed many gifts. He described to David the responses of the prisoners and the joy they experienced for being remembered.

Hours passed and Frankie relaxed. As the plane landed, the crew led the passengers in a Hebrew song of joy, and Frankie joined in clapping and singing.

The group went to the Garden Tomb on their first afternoon in Israel. Standing in front of the empty tomb, Frankie preached a beautiful sermon to sixty-four of his fellow travelers. Eyes swelled with tears as he told them how he personally met the resurrected Christ. Jesus reached out and made Himself known to Frankie at a time when he was bound in chains, alone, and crying; Jesus set him free and placed him in his own Jerusalem at the South Carolina state penitentiary. As the travelers left the Garden Tomb, Frankie radiated his joy and peace like never before.

One day, two buses full of travelers ventured to the Augusta Victoria Hospital on the Mount of Olives and the Crippled Children's Hospital. Frankie dressed in his Easter bunny costume and sang and danced for the children and nurses; then he presented each one with a cup of candy. What a hilarious sight he was in those red pants and shirt from his Santa suit and long ears and a carrot dangling as his tail from his Easter bunny suit. The children laughed and shouted as Frankie hopped around the room and brought love and joy from America.

The customs inspectors and airline personnel had been puzzled by Frankie's luggage though. When they had opened his bags, they were shocked at the colorful attire. They checked every seam in his Easter bunny suit and his funny puppets. They examined every pocket and even inspected the carrot.

At every inspection stop, the carrot was very carefully pinched and squeezed. If only they could have seen the children, they would have understood.

Every day in Israel was filled with new adventures as the group went from one biblical site to another. When they stopped at the house of Caiaphas, the high priest, however, Frankie's heart broke. This was where Jesus had been held prisoner on the night of His betrayal and arrest. In the dungeon and pit where Jesus had been unjustly confined, Frankie wept, openly and unashamedly. Jesus also knew the sorrow of being in prison. Is that why His heavenly presence is so special in prisons? One must wonder.

When the travelers went to Bethlehem, they saw a flock of sheep in the Shepherd's Field. True to his nature, Frankie donned a shepherd's hat, took his shepherd's flute, and went among the sheep to have his picture taken. The sight of a Japanese shepherd in a crazy hat making weird sounds with his flute was too much even for the sheep. They scattered to all directions and left Frankie alone for his picture. No matter what, he kept all of his fellow travelers laughing and crying for the entire tour.

The group also visited the Church of the Nativity where Christ was born. They descended a steep staircase to arrive at the manger. Frankie's heart pounded against his chest with emotion. Because Christmas had been so meaningful to him, it is little wonder that he was moved at this sight. They gathered around the manger, prayed, and sang. At the end, Frankie broke out into his Japanese version of "Silent Night." Even the priests upstairs who typically paid no attention to tourists left their stations and went down to listen. So touched were all present that Frankie's Christmas was in his heart – every day.[62]

---

62   Adapted from "Frankie San Goes to Bethlehem," by David R. Barnhart, *Cell 55*, 1975.

Last Farewell

When Frankie left Tokyo in 1961, his parents did not understand, but they accepted that he had given his life to Jesus and was determined to follow Him. Frankie loved and respected his parents but knew he had to move on. Years passed and Frankie voluntarily lived with the thieves and murderers because he sensed their silent, desperate cries. He had lost his old life but found his spiritual life. *We know love by this, that He laid down His life for us; and we ought to lay down our lives for the brethren* (1 John 3:16).

Frankie's father reminded him that he would always be welcomed home; he still did not understand Frankie's life among the tough characters. His mother encouraged him with his decision. She knew his commitment and stubborn determination; she saw a rough life ahead, the grief, the frustration, and the loneliness, but she believed in him. She was right too. Frankie did shed blood, sweat, and tears in his unusual life, but he had also made his parents very happy.

Frankie corresponded regularly with his mother, and both of his parents recognized how much they missed him. He had not seen his mother since 1964, but in 1968 his father came to visit him. However, that was the year of the riots – one of which broke out the day after he arrived. Frankie quickly sent him home where he would be safe.

Frankie's desire was to see his parents one more time before they passed away, just to say a last farewell, but the prison work and weekend speaking engagements kept him busy all of the time. So Frankie delayed making plans to travel back to Japan, leaving that up to the Lord.

Soon after Christmas that year (about twenty years after Frankie's arrival), he received an invitation to speak at a conference in Los Angeles, which is about a third of the way to Japan.

Frankie was surprised because he had never been invited to speak so far from South Carolina, but he realized that the Lord knew he missed his parents and had waited a long time to visit them. He made arrangements to speak at the conference – then head onward to Japan.

Before leaving, Frankie visited those on death row and was thankful there had been no executions. However, one was scheduled for while he was gone, so he promptly determined he would have to delay the trip back to Japan. At the last minute, this prisoner received a stay of execution, so Frankie returned to his original plans and headed for Japan.

Frankie knew fathers and mothers desire happiness for their children. Jesus teaches children to love and honor their parents, so he wanted to share his love with them before they were gone.[63]

---

63   Adapted from "Last Farewell," by Frankie San, *Cell 55*, 1981.

Chapter 15

Thoughts from Death Row

Frankie visited the men on death row at least once a week – sometimes more. He sat on the cement floor and talked to them, sharing and crying with them as he built a relationship and trust; then he could eventually introduce them to Christ. When asked why he spent his time with men who had no future, he said, "How do these 'unforgiven' receive the Lord and His forgiveness if we do not minister to them?"

One morning the associate warden called Frankie and said, "Frankie, I think we're going to have a disturbance among the death row inmates. We still have to let them out, but I think they're plotting something." On this segregated unit, the inmates were free to roam the cellblock each day. The warden wanted Frankie to do something.

Frankie replied, "Okay. Just wait and give me about thirty minutes." Frankie ran to the nearby grocery store and bought fruit, ice cream, and cookies. When he got back, he said, "I am ready. Put up a table over here and there." As the inmates started coming out, he told them, "We're going to have a Bingo party." So they did. They ate their ice cream and cookies and forgot about the disturbance. By touching their humanity and treating them with compassion, Frankie defused a potential riot.

One condemned man whom Frankie came to know as a brother told him that "through the Lord I have learned to see the electric chair not as an end, but as a door. My life will not end in the death house; it will begin there. My Lord will open a new door."

It is sad that this man did not learn of Jesus and the salvation that He purchased before he ended up on death row, but thanks to Frankie, he did hear and he believed. As long as a man is breathing, the possibility exists for him to understand the salvation that God offers and accept that gospel.

Tommy's Predicament

Frankie had visited Tommy in the Maximum Detention Retraining Center and brought him soap and towels at a time when Tommy was in great need. Frankie asked him what he'd like for Christmas, and Tommy wrote to him and said:

> I would appreciate anything that you would want to give me because when you are in a place like this, you will be glad to get what you can, but I don't want you to stick you [sic] neck out for me as trying to help me out of the security building because I am not worth it. I am not the same Tommy that were [sic] in your classroom years ago. . . . You have heard of all the things I have done, shooting at officers in towers, jumping over prison walls.
>
> And I know you wonder what made me do some of the evil things that I have did [sic]. Being behind

bars all the time gives you a feeling you got to be free or die. And right now I have a very high tempo (temper). I can make up my mind right now to go back to CCI and make my time trying my best not to get into trouble, and turn around and walk right into trouble because I can't control my tempo. And then I might go out there and never get into anything. But someday I will be leaving this joint for good. I personally feel that I would feel like a fish out of water after my release.

There was more in Tommy's letter, but this much depicts the hopelessness that he was feeling. This letter was a cry for help, and Frankie wanted to find a way to make him believe he was a worthwhile human being. Frankie wanted all of the men to understand that the Lord offers forgiveness and a new way of life.

Another convict, Jack, read Tommy's letter and was moved by the despair. Jack had been in prison for seventeen years – awaiting execution on death row for robbery and murder. Because of this, he believed he was qualified to respond to Tommy's letter. He said:

> This man, considered one of the toughest and most dangerous prisoners here, is more a frightened child than the tough con he has been labeled. I pray that our Lord will guide us to the knowledge that will make it possible to show men such as this that they can be good, and that they can live in society and not feel like a fish out of water. . . . But society must accept His guidance. I am not a Bible scholar, but I know that Jesus said to minister to the sick not the healthy. What man needs

ministering more than the sick soul who says, "I
am no good."

My own life might have been saved and made use-
ful, but there was no hand to reach out when I was
frightened and in need of comfort. Perhaps I might
have been a good person if someone had shown
me the meaning of the "living gospel." I read the
Bible and the tracts and heard the people running
around saying, "God loves you." But that is not the
living gospel as I have come to know it. To me, loving our Lord is to love every man; it is to share his
burden; it is to minister to the sick; and it is also to
give hope to those who have none.

Walls, fences, bars, and dark cells will not bring
men to know and love our Lord Jesus. Christians
must beat down these barriers and spread the news
of salvation to these forgotten men. "No good?"
Man was created in the image of God; there is
good in every man.[64]

Though Jack did not say he saw the living gospel in Frankie,
many others did. Frankie knew that the way he lived his life
and what the prisoners saw in him was more important than
any words he might preach at them. Frankie loved these men
– his brothers.

Conversion and Remorse

Yes, conversion can take place on death row, and it does. The
prisoner's perspective changes immensely. Frankie spoon-fed
the message of Christmas to Robert one sip at a time. After

---

64   Excerpt from *Cell 55*, January 1976.

forty-one years, Robert said, "It was better than any feast a king might have served. . . . I know that I have a long way to go yet. Death row is a great weight that I have to carry each day. But the load is lighter now that I have invited Jesus into my life. I now see what is important; each day now has meaning whereas before there was only void."

Another inmate described his remorse this way:

> I actually hate myself. I live each day with constant replays in my head. I think about the two dead victims; then I think about their daughter who was left without a mom or dad – because of me. I think about the victims' families, all the hell that I put them through. For many generations to come, I affected their families – also for my family, especially my two kids and my ex-wife.
>
> I made the wrong decision, and instantly I went from no trouble to one of the worst people in the state. It was like a chain reaction. I'm not okay with what went down, but I never denied my crimes. Every day, it's like a knife against my throat or a knife in my heart. . . . There is one thing I know that can't be taken away from me: the love of my Lord and Savior. . . . I know without God we are nothing. . . . God died so we could live – to be in His presence instead of in torment and suffering forever.

James wrote, "The main thing to remember is that even if all my earthly avenues fail and they do eventually execute me, it wouldn't matter because I know that I am saved through our Lord Jesus Christ, and to be absent from the body is to be present with the Lord. As long as I cling to Christ through faith, I can't lose."

Though some inmates try to excuse themselves, not all do; some see their violence for the sin and destruction it is. Sometimes these acts of violence are the result of a life of crime; often they are not. Sometime the crimes are the result of a lifetime of abuse – abuse that is internalized until it explodes and destroys other lives. Too often crimes are due to a drug-crazed individual or mental instability. No matter what the cause of the crime, Frankie concentrated on loving the prisoners and helping them move their lives in a positive direction. Some, certainly not all, found a Savior in the process.

Chapter 16

Broad River Correctional Institution

As word got out that the South Carolina Central Correctional Institution was closing, many of Frankie's friends wrote to encourage him in his work but more so to congratulate him for a work well done. They expressed how they knew he would be missed because so many of the guys were quite attached to him. They thanked him for showing them the "right way" and teaching them right from wrong.

Some even thanked Frankie for sending them his *Cell 55* newsletters and commented that they read them over and over. Many said they were homesick for him. Essentially, they knew that the closing of CCI and losing Frankie with his library would be like losing an historical symbol. There would never again be a Frankie's "oasis."

The first move came in January 1990, when death row inmates moved from the then 123-year-old Central Correctional Institution to the new facility a few miles away – Broad River Correctional Institution. Forty-six death row inmates, Frankie's friends, quietly transferred to this new institution, a move that they had anxiously awaited. They left the noise, the crumbling walls, and the subpar food. They also left Frankie. In the new facility, other organizations and volunteers visited and gave them special attention, so he thought it best to watch over the 1,350 men left in the run-down prison.

Even so, he had developed close relationships with some of the death row inmates and saying good-bye was difficult. He knew the officers were cautious, but they treated his friends in a professional way. The inmates were nervous too. Frankie gave them time to become acquainted and meet their new librarian.

Within a week, Robert wrote a note to Frankie and told him that each cell had a window. He had seen a star – the first one he had seen in several years. He also said the food was better and the guards treated them well. Tears filled Frankie's eyes as he read the note. He thanked the Lord again for Robert and for the improved conditions for these men.

After a couple months, Frankie had an opportunity to visit his transplanted friends. He saw the nice cells and enjoyed the relaxed, friendly atmosphere. The men could leave their cells and play games around a table or lift weights. One inmate even coaxed Frankie into a game of handball in the yard. Frankie and his partner lost. He thought maybe he was too old for that game but refused to admit that.

Though they had been few, executions were very hard for Frankie. He knew these men had committed inexcusable, horrible crimes, but as he spent time with them and got to know them personally, they became friends. He experienced extreme trauma and emotional anguish; a bit of Frankie died with each execution. God helped him endure and gave him spiritual courage to continue His prison mission work.

From the beginning, Frankie knew he would suffer and struggle among the oppressed prisoners, but he also found the real meaning of life among them. He knew the Holy Spirit was at work as he heard the still small voice: *To the extent that you did it to one of these brothers of Mine, even the least of them, you did it to Me* (Matthew 25:40). Frankie knew God was there in the dungeon with them and *in Him was life, and the life was the Light of men* (John 1:4).

In his own words, Frankie wrote, "I thank the Lord that He let me complete this chapter of the story of CCI this year. I am not sure what He'll assign to me next after the closing of this 127-year-old prison. Whatever He will appoint for me is fine with me, and I'll carry on His task as long as I live, and I'll make a joyful noise to God and serve the Lord with gladness. Emmanuel – God is with us – indeed in the darkest of prisons."[65]

In the words of his former roommate, Peter Setzer, the enormity of the work that Frankie accomplished in the prison is evident:

> "Now you've arrived victorious at the end of a long, incredibly difficult, and faithful ministry. . . . All the rest of the seminary class have served two or three, even four parishes. You have the longest single tenure of us all. You stuck it out to the end. You survived and thousands of prisoners have had a glimpse of Christ in the middle of hell. Some have been saved, snatched from the quicksand. . . . *Well done, good and faithful slave* (Matthew 25:21)."

As CCI closed, Frankie lost his home. He had lived on the prison site for the entire twenty-eight years he worked there. With the closing, he had nowhere to go. He had never owned a home and had no idea what to do, but the Lord knew. He provided Frankie with a cozy condominium of his own, through his parents in Tokyo.

---

65   Adapted from newsletter, *The Year of Our Lord 1993*.

Chapter 17

Life after CCI

A New Mission

The ancient prison had been scheduled to permanently close all its doors in November of 1993. However, that was postponed until the spring of 1994. Frankie still did not know what God had for him next, but he waited. During that time, an inmate came to him because he didn't know who else to go to. He had AIDS.

This poor soul was dirty and smelly; his eyes were bloodshot and tears rolled down his cheeks. Frankie's first impression was that he was an addict and needed money, but he only wanted to have someone listen to him. Frankie discovered he was face to face with the disease he had been hearing so much about. He did not know how to help this man, but they talked and talked. For the time that CCI was still open, Frankie gave him a job at the library.

Frankie had heard that some of the inmates had this very dreadful disease, but he didn't know who they were. At this point, he needed to decide how he could help this man. What would Jesus do? Unknown to Frankie, he was coming to a turning point in his life once again. Frankie recalled how the apostle Paul could rejoice while in prison awaiting his own execution but still share the good news of Jesus Christ. He could say, *Rejoice in the Lord always; again I will say, rejoice!* (Philippians 4:4).

Because of his encounter with this man, Frankie announced that he was moving on to a new work. He would help those with AIDS. He would assist with a support group and teach the young the dangers involved with the feared disease – a disease that did not discriminate by race, religion, wealth, or poverty.

Before leaving CCI, Frankie's concern for those with HIV/AIDS grew. He knew that the South Carolina Department of Corrections offered good medical care, but there was no program to offer emotional or spiritual support to these dying men. Frankie discussed his concerns with Parker Evatt, the SCDC commissioner. At first, he was reluctant to have Frankie become involved in caring for terminally ill inmates, but after much discussion and prayer, he agreed to have Frankie work with these men on a full-time basis.

The next question was, could Frankie survive watching his inmate patients/friends die – one after another, week after week? Only God knew – only God could give him the strength. The first year was very difficult as he watched these desperately ill men pass away, one after another. He felt so helpless – almost like he was suffocating. But he could not abandon them; he was all that many of them had. He held their hands as they lay dying alone in prison. He knew someone had to lead them to Jesus Christ – even at this late point in their lives.

Frankie persevered through the pain and struggle and gained a deeper satisfaction in his life than at any other time. Though past retirement age, he continued to serve Jesus and those with AIDS. From the Kirkland Correctional Institution he could visit anyone he wanted to – even those in other prisons and those on death row. The one place he was not allowed to visit was the cold, hard, sterile maximum security unit at Kirkland where even the cockroaches feared to tread.

Frankie could correspond with these men, however, and three of them did exactly that. Two even shared their faith in the Lord from there. The fact that the Lord can reach lost souls in such a horrible place encouraged him. Yes, Jesus was working among them.

Christmas at Kirkland

Frankie settled into his work and by Christmas 1995, he was in full swing with his normal festivities. After his very first Christmas at CCI, when he had nothing to give the prisoners but himself, Frankie labored to bring joy and love to those forgotten men. Every year had seemed better than the last and included more facilities and more people.

The Christmas program in 1995 started with a visit on the first Sunday of December to the state mental institution where Frankie sang with thirty-five patients. After that he ran back and forth between Kmart, Walmart, and the farmer's market to purchase what he needed to provide another successful program. He bought 35 cases of bananas, 12 cases of apples, 1,000 bags of candy, and 8 boxes of shower shoes. With these items, he was able to bring gifts to 1,000 inmates and patients – small gifts for Christmas, a gesture of human kindness. Quite a difference from that first sad, lonely Christmas behind bars.

Some of the inmates at Kirkland did not know Frankie yet or realize the love that came from the Japanese Santa. A few made derogatory remarks and complained of the quantity, size, or color of their gifts, but none of them refused them. In their hearts, they were thankful that someone cared enough to give them something. However, later in the year one inmate wrote, "I received a toothbrush, toothpaste, soap, washcloth, writing pad, stamps, and two packs of Life Savers candy. I used everything thankfully and sparingly for six months; but the Life Savers, which I enjoyed once a day, did not hold out."[66]

Santa's helpers always seemed to receive the best gift of all – the opportunity to sweat from the work of Christmas preparations and see the smiles and joy of the inmates who realized they had been remembered. As Santa and his helpers collapsed from exhaustion, they were blessed from above for taking Christmas love to the forgotten men.

Frankie's last stop of the season was at the Lowman Old Folks Home where some of the seniors didn't quite know what to think of a Japanese Santa who sang and danced around the room. Santa enjoyed the time immensely as he sang:

> Go, tell it on the mountain,
>> Over the hills and everywhere;
> Go, tell it on the mountain,
>> That Jesus Christ is born.[67]

The following year, however, when Frankie asked the warden for permission to conduct his annual Christmas program, he did not get approval. That compelled Frankie to go over his head and make the request directly to the SCDC. Thanksgiving came and went. No response. Frankie feared that for the first time he'd have to cancel his program. But just a couple weeks before Christmas, the approval came and relief flooded through Frankie.

With so little time, Frankie had to move fast to gather all that he needed. The first week he rushed around making purchases and arrangements. The second week he delivered care packages to eighteen hundred men with bananas, candy, cups

---

66   Adapted from newsletter from Christmas 1996.
67   "Go Tell It on the Mountain," Anonymous, 1907, *www*.library.timelesstruths. org/music/Go_Tell_It_on_the _Mountain.

of instant soup, and pads of writing paper. It wasn't much, but for many of them, it was all they would get. Many were alone in this world. One such inmate wrote and said, "A lot of us don't have any families . . . but we have you, Frankie, and that means a lot. You give us hope, understanding, and compassion. And that is what will save a lot of us and turn our lives around. I know it has worked for me."

Hospice Expands

Many of the inmates spent decades of their lives in and out of prisons – and sometimes just in for life. Lifelong friendships developed with some of them as they ended up in the same facilities time after time. Charles (Animal) was one of the in-and-outers. When CCI closed, he was moved to Broad River Correctional Institution where he saw his old friend Ronnie, though he did not recognize him at first. When Ronnie told him who he was, Charles felt like he had been hit with a baseball bat. He had known Ronnie as the strongest, most vibrant man at CCI. Now he was a walking skeleton standing on shaking legs. When Charles asked what had happened to him, he was further shocked to learn that Ronnie had full-blown AIDS.

After a couple weeks, Charles was asked to help with some of Ronnie's care, so he took turns with Joe to make sure Ronnie had what he needed. As the work of caring for him increased, Charles approached Frankie to pull a string or two to allow him to be a hospice care worker for Ronnie full-time. Frankie managed to get Charles on the inmate medical staff – inmate helping inmate.

Charles had no idea how hard the job would be. He pushed the wheelchair, helped him drink, and fixed food for him. He dealt with Ronnie's emotions, fears, and even resentfulness. It was a trial for both of them, but Charles said, "I must thank you, Frankie San, because you were my strength when I so often didn't think I could go on. Watching you come in each week and knowing that this was just one of your many stops, seeing you smile and laugh as if this person was the only one in the world, gave me the strength to keep going back to help this one man."

As with many experiences in life, Frankie believed that Ronnie's last days and death helped Charles come to the Lord. But surely, this situation also indicated that one hospice worker could not care for all of the terminal patients. This program was destined to expand.[68]

In his humble way, Frankie did what he could as he saw the needs. One day he went to visit an inmate who was rapidly succumbing to the AIDS virus. The man asked Frankie to bring him some grapes, so Frankie returned that night with the grapes and fed some to him. That small act of kindness brought happiness and gratefulness to that poor sick man. Twenty-four hours later, he passed away.

Another time as Frankie walked down the hallway of the prison hospital, he heard someone calling, "Hot! Hot! Hot!" He entered the room and discovered how hot and stuffy it was. The man was so miserable that Frankie told him he would try to get the air conditioner turned on, but the nurses told him the whole cooling system had broken down. So Frankie went to the store and bought a small fan. When he returned, he found the man lying silently with his eyes closed. Sweat trickled down his face. Frankie plugged the fan in and directed it toward him. His eyes opened and he cried in relief, "Air! Air!" He nodded at Frankie and closed his eyes again. In the morning, he too had passed away.

One terminally ill patient was so depressed he refused to eat anything. The nurse told Frankie that he only had a short

---

68   Adapted from newsletter from Christmas 1996.

prison sentence, but if he didn't eat, he would not make it home. The man refused to talk to Frankie; he just stared at the gray wall next to his bed. Frankie told him he would get him something good to eat and returned later with bananas, plums, and doughnuts. He quietly put them on the table next to him and left. When he peeked in later, he was overjoyed to see him eating some of the food.[69]

All of these special acts of kindness and errands took their toll on Frankie. After four years of this ministry, he felt overwhelmed by the sheer number of sick and dying men. So many dying and so little that he was able to do to ease their suffering. Frankie was increasingly exhausted mentally and spiritually. He had no one to turn to, no one to talk to about these dying inmates. Caring for criminals was not popular, but as a follower of Christ, Frankie had been called to love his fellow man, not judge him. He had to turn to the Lord for comfort and guidance. Would He hear?

Enter John Lunn

One day while visiting inmates in the infirmary, a man walked up to Frankie. "Are you Frankie San?" he asked. "I've heard much about you." He shook Frankie's hand and told him his name was John Lunn. He explained that he had been hired by the department to set up and organize a hospice care program.

Frankie stared at him. Speechless. Did he say hospice program? This John-something was to be a hospice organizer? Frankie had not heard of such a thing – completely out of the blue! Sort of. Throughout his thirty-two years of ministry, Frankie had seen many times how the Lord removed obstacles and came to his aid when he needed Him most. One more time he witnessed the love and provision of His grace. God saw his

---

69   Adapted from *Advent Newsletter 1997*, by Frankie San.

need. He heard his cry. He sent an "angel" named John Lunn to rescue Frankie at a most needful time.

Later, John came back to Frankie and told him he was ready to set up hospice care programs at several facilities. As a registered nurse and ordained minister, John proved wise, insightful, and capable in drawing up a plan. He wanted Frankie to help train inmate volunteers who could assist the medical staff in caring for the terminally ill patients. How great a vision – giving inmates an important purpose in their lives as they served their fellow inmates.

Together, John and Frankie set up these programs in seven different facilities. They trained more than eighty inmates to be volunteers. In this way, they provided spiritual, physical, and emotional support to dying men in prison. They received twenty-five hours of training and enjoyed a graduation ceremony at the end where they received a certificate and celebrated with a small reception.

During the training sessions, Frankie served goodies such as bananas, cheese, nuts, oranges, grapes, croissants, and doughnuts. These not only brought smiles to the inmates in training but also showed them they were special to be involved in this important work. Treating them this way showed them respect. He shared stories and pictures of his ministry and described how he had served the terminally ill men when the AIDS crisis occurred. Frankie noted the deep hunger in the eyes of the volunteers who wanted to be part of something good and noble. Obviously, they would benefit from the program also. Offering compassion and kindness has a way of changing the lives of the giver and the receiver.[70]

When one of these volunteers reported for his first assignment, he tried to smile when he saw his patient and thought to himself, "Frankie and John, what have you gotten me into

70   Adapted from "Prison Hospice Ministry," by John Lunn, *Cell 55*, Spring 1998.

now?" He quickly learned the not-so-pleasant aspects of caring for the patient's needs; he changed his diaper, helped him shower, and brushed his teeth. Then he read to him. Though the man tried to bite him one day in the shower, he persevered. Then one day as he was leaving, his patient told him, "You are the only one who cares." In prison that is often the case.

Chapter 18

Retirement

How does one retire from a lifelong ministry? In 1998, when Frankie decided it was time to officially retire from full-time work, he hoped to continue with part-time work. He requested to be allowed to work with terminally ill patients, so within one week of his "retirement," he was back to work with the inmates.

Frankie's ministry became especially important when the prison officials in South Carolina had all the inmates tested for HIV. Over six hundred inmates tested positive, and these were living in the general population of prisoners. Little was known about how the disease spread at that time, so the director decided to separate them by moving them to the Broad River prison, right next door to Frankie's infirmary at the Kirkland prison.

On May 1, 2001, the budget axe fell, and Frankie's position disappeared. The timing seemed all wrong, and he wondered why the Lord had not answered his prayer to continue serving Him in the prison. Other retirees spent time with children, grandchildren, and great-grandchildren. Frankie's "children" were in prison. What was he to do? He couldn't very well carry around pictures of tattoo-covered murderers and bank robbers to show his friends. So, on the day of his termination, he asked permission to visit the inmates as a volunteer.

With the close proximity of the prison, visiting them in the mess hall worked well for Frankie. He already knew many of them, so he walked over at noon and headed for the cafeteria. Frankie was dismayed when he saw the arrangements for lunch in the cafeteria. In the area where the food was served, a metal partition had been installed to screen the workers and food from the inmates. At the bottom of the partition was a ten-inch-high glass window through which the prisoners selected their food. It was then passed through a small opening at the end. The fear of AIDS caused workers to treat the inmates in less than human ways – more like animals.

When the first group of prisoners finished, the second group appeared. Frankie saw how sad and humiliated they looked. Their families and loved ones had deserted them; now they were segregated from the general prison population. They hung their heads, didn't talk to one another, and shuffled through the line. All of a sudden, one of them shouted, "Hey, Frankie! Frankie, you're here! Glad to see you!"

Frankie hurried over to James, shook his hand, and hugged him tightly. Soon others called out to Frankie. Some smiled and laughed. Frankie sat and ate lunch with his friends and exchanged stories. He was so overjoyed to see so many of his old friends that he decided to return the next day. However, the next day Frankie noticed that the tables were not cleaned off. The kitchen workers would not come out until all AIDS inmates were finished eating.

Astonished by this situation, Frankie grabbed a cloth and some water and washed fifty-four tables before the next group arrived. He repeated that four times. Two hundred and sixteen tables in an hour and a half are a lot of tables to clean, but Frankie knew that lunchtime was the best opportunity to see these men. He wiped tables and cleaned the floor while he chatted with them and grabbed a few bites for himself. Frankie was thrilled with the new door that the Lord had opened for him to serve, and he considered it even better than his work before retirement. He said, "Jesus has fulfilled my life with one great assignment after another, but working among these lonely, forsaken HIV/AIDS inmates is the greatest gift and best assignment He has ever given to me."[71]

One last desire remained for Frankie. Harry's name kept popping into his head, and he wanted to see him. Harry had been assisting with the legal cases of many of the inmates in CCI, and after many years of wandering, he accepted the Lord. He then took Bible correspondence courses and was active among fellow believers. As Frankie felt his own purpose fading away, the Lord brought Harry back to him, and life was still worthwhile after that forced retirement. If he had still been working, he would not have had much free time to spend with Harry and see him grow and work among the inmates. Harry joyfully spread the good news among his fellow prisoners, and another chapter began in Frankie's life.

As Frankie faced the reality of his retirement, he had these words to say:

> My ministry these many long years has been trying
> to redeem human lives that the rest of the world
> has given up on. . . . When I reflect on all the lives I
> have been able to touch, I am so honored that God
> chose me for this sacred mission. And every time
> I witness another seemingly irrevocably lost soul
> turn to embrace the love of our Lord and Savior,
> I know what it feels like to win an Olympic gold
> medal, but mine is the most important gold medal

---

71   Frankie San's Prison Ministry Report, 1998.

in life. *I have fought the good fight, I have finished the course, I have kept the faith* (2 Timothy 4:7).

David

Many people do not understand Frankie's love for these incarcerated men. Some even disagreed with the compassion that he showed them, and they criticized him for it. In later years, when Frankie was living in a condominium, David was his neighbor. David was not interested in reading *Cell 55*; he took a copy – but returned it the next day and told Frankie he didn't care to read the prisoners' stories. For a long time, Frankie didn't mention the prison work, and David was okay with that.

One day as the two of them discussed a newspaper article about crime and worsening prison conditions, Frankie told David more about his work. David responded, "These prisoners are fed three square meals a day, and the doctor takes care of them when they get sick, while poor folks in society are having a tough time getting medicines and food themselves. We should lock four or six guys in a cell – I don't care. They asked for it and they got it. Lock them up and throw away the key!"

"You don't know anything about prison and its prisoners," Frankie shouted. "You can leave right now – get out of here. Out, out, out!" He was quite angry.

David got up and left, slamming the door behind him. A few days later, he appeared on Frankie's doorstep with some homemade soup for him – a peace offering that cooled the turbulence between them. One morning as Frankie stepped out to get his newspaper, he found two pieces of typewritten paper attached to his door.

On these pages, David described in a story how similar he was to Frankie. Both men rose early. Both faced the days with anticipation. Both left their homes before sunrise to go fishing

– David for striped bass, Frankie for souls. David was disillusioned with the churches and church people. He said they were generous at Thanksgiving and Christmas, but they forgot the hungry the rest of the year. But then he looked at his own life and realized he was no different.

David had watched Frankie get up in the wee hours of the morning to visit the farmer's market. He saw Frankie buy huge boxes of apples, bananas, and oranges, and unload them all into his house to keep them fresh until the next day when he'd take them to the thieves, murderers, and rapists whom he loved. David said it took him a couple years to understand that Frankie was teaching them about Jesus – and he was teaching David too.

One day David picked up his Bible, and the words seemed to jump off the page at him – in red letters! Everything Jesus told them to do was being lived out next door to him. He concluded his story with these words: "Can I live as Frankie San lives? No, I cannot – it's too hard. But I do thank God for His grace and for sending His Son to save a wretch like me. Loving Jesus, loving this country, loving His sheep, and loving life in general, he denies himself for others . . . 'The Lord gave him a life sentence.' He is a lifer. . . . Frankie San is the happiest person I know."[72]

However, Frankie said:

> The Bible teaches us to help these people, the least
> of the brethren. The apostle Paul said, *Do not*
> *be overcome by evil, but overcome evil with good*
> (Romans 12:21). . . . Regardless of what people might
> say, it really doesn't matter. These men in prison are in
> agony . . . and Jesus said to love your neighbor as your-
> self. . . . Many of those incarcerated men will never get

---

72   Adapted from *Cell 55*, Summer 2009.

out for what they've done, but I don't leave them there to rot. Instead, I try to help them find freedom from their bondage by introducing them to Jesus Christ, so they might stand firm in life regardless of their circumstances. . . . I can honestly tell you that I have peace in my heart, knowing that I am doing what God called me to do.

Frankie's Plea to America

Frankie witnessed great changes in our country, the one he always referred to as "this great nation." He watched young people go to prison rather than fight in the Vietnam War. He watched the failures of Presidents Nixon and Clinton. But the worst was when someone declared, "Character does not matter as long as the job is accomplished." He saw this philosophy infect another whole generation. Frankie believed that if character fails, all of society will collapse. When character doesn't matter, right or wrong don't matter either, and the family disintegrates. Children have no one to teach them of God, so God does not become a stabilizing force in their lives. The result is that children do not understand right from wrong, and many join gangs to have a close connection with others. Men end up in prison and actually want help, but don't necessarily receive it.

Frankie witnessed the losing battle of prison reform. Though the officials had attempted to implement forms of rehabilitation, most of them lacked spiritual rebuilding. Without that, the recidivism of prisoners was great. They might obtain physical freedom, but without spiritual freedom, moral freedom, and a new character, they could not make it outside the walls. Without the Lord and His purpose in their lives, they quickly fell back into their old habits with their old friends. Or, without any friends or family, they soon became homeless and turned to crime to survive.

Certain programs like education, life skills, pre-release planning, job/vocational skills, and cultural sensitivity had proved beneficial. Without these, a released inmate had nowhere to turn for employment, and the vicious cycle of crime repeated itself. While the men were incarcerated, Frankie could provide a positive mental and spiritual example. He could change their attitudes but not their character, and that was not enough. He found he could do nothing to change their character except through the Lord Jesus Christ.

One former addict wrote to Frankie that he knew Frankie could not change his character. He knew that would only come from the Lord, and he encouraged Frankie to keep teaching the value and importance of character.

Another wrote to tell Frankie that he had received Jesus into his life and had quit smoking, drinking, and messing with drugs. He had found a peace like he had never known before. He knew that with Jesus in his heart, he could make the right choices even when it was hard.

After September 11, 2001, Frankie considered the similarities between that day and Pearl Harbor. He knew that the country needed to be aware of the external threat of terrorists, but he had also observed for over four decades that our greatest threat came from within. America had prospered economically and allowed itself to be lulled into a false sense of security with material gain, while its spiritual and moral foundations had eroded. He saw Americans lose their focus on God as they embraced multiculturalism and diversity. This introduced the concept of moral relativism where right and wrong do not exist. There is no truth – or it cannot be known. Frankie summarized the deterioration of America in one of his newsletters:

Because our nation is composed of people from widely diverse cultural and ethnic groups, each having its own unique value system or ethical code, we seem to have concluded that there is no such thing as "truth" or moral certitude. In the final analysis, anything goes. Somehow the existence of many different standards proves that there is no standard. Amoralists and atheists are attracted to that position and promote it with vigor. They say nothing is really right or wrong. What is true depends entirely on one's point of view. The highest form of good, therefore, is tolerance to anything and everything except traditional Christianity, which is the chief source of what they call intolerance.

Frankie believed the obvious and most important front on which the battle for faith is being waged is within the family. The ever-increasing number of young people in prison proves that Americans have lost sight of the moral compass to guide them. Our first line of defense should be in the homes and schools and should be grounded on teachings from the Bible. Frankie saw that instead of teaching about God's love, we have left the children to learn for themselves, as parents work harder to gain more material goods and self-reliance.

[If] My people who are called by My name humble themselves and pray and seek My face and turn from their wicked ways, then I will hear from heaven, will forgive their sin and will heal their land. (2 Chronicles 7:14)

Frankie's plea for America was to rethink our priorities in order to place God back first in our lives and turn our attention to our families. God is not dead. "Our Judeo-Christian heritage has been under attack by those who wish to do away with God, resulting in the disillusion of our younger citizens."[73] He maintained that people needed to wake up to their responsibilities to bring their children up in the nurture and admonition of the Lord. Frankie taught that only Christ has the answer to the sin problem. Without Him, families fail, and the underlying structure of society crumbles.

---

73   Adapted from *Cell 55*, Summer 2005.

Chapter 19

Passing the Torch

As Frankie's activity slowed down, his students, both inmates and free men, stepped up to the plate and carried on the work of taking the gospel to any who needed it, but particularly to the forgotten men. Through these men, Frankie's work continued and spread.

In 2003, however, Frankie wrote:

> As much passion as I had for the Lord in serving Him through the forgotten lives of the prisoners, I finally reached a point of exhaustion. The passing of my dear friend and next-door neighbor, coupled with the loss of my mother a few months later, sent me in a downward spiral of emotional plight. I simply had no energy to leave my bed and go on my visitations. As I tried to get up, the day seemed so gloomy and I had no joy in my heart. I fell back into bed thinking that perhaps I had worn myself out. So I remained there.
>
> I realized that like so many of the men I had served

behind the walls, I too had become institutionalized. But I had no counsel. No one had experienced
what I had. The cross had become too heavy, and I
cried out to the Lord.

Then . . . it happened again! The Lord sent a young
stranger to rescue me from my predicament. He
had done it again.

One night at Kinkos, a young man approached Frankie and
introduced himself. He had been a correctional officer at the
Broad River Correctional Institution, so they shared prison
experiences. God used this to change Frankie's life one more
time. He gained energy, felt renewed, and became involved in
street ministry.

The Christmas programs in the prisons were nearing their
end, and sometimes permission to visit and give gifts was hard
to get. Frankie had never been able to mingle at his friends'
family gatherings at Christmas. The strenuous emotional invest-
ment with the inmates was too great to turn his back and join
in the merriment outside the walls. But he had no desire to go
anywhere else, not even back to Japan. He said, "What would I
do? Live with my family and run a restaurant? . . . In America I
was able to give myself fully over to God for this special work."

All through these years Frankie gave his time, counsel, and
love. His presence was like a caring doctor who meticulously
worked to cure an ailing patient. And through his service, some
of the men discovered the secret to loving that was right before
their eyes: Frankie had loved them as God loved them, regardless of their past. He taught them the truth that the apostle Paul
gave the Ephesians:

*Be kind to one another, tender-hearted, forgiving
each other, just as God in Christ also has forgiven
you. Therefore be imitators of God, as beloved
children; and walk in love, just as Christ also
loved you and gave Himself up for us, an offering and a sacrifice to God as a fragrant aroma.*
(Ephesians 4:32-5:2)

Harry

Harry was one of those the Lord sent to assist and carry on
Frankie's work. He was a former engineer and Vietnam veteran
who had turned to drugs and ultimately ended up in prison.
He worked for Frankie in the law library, but when CCI closed,
Harry was transferred. After many years of contact, loss of contact, and reconnection, he became Frankie's spiritual partner
behind bars. After sixteen years, he saw God's truth and committed his life to Jesus Christ. He read the Bible, took courses in
Greek and Hebrew, and became actively involved in Christian
activities within the prison faith community.

Even though Frankie retired, he met with Harry every day
for a devotional and visitation time. Harry related to him how
his fellow prisoners did not understand the good news that
he was trying to convey. Frankie told him, "Here, take this
candy to them and say 'Jesus loves you.'" So Harry did that
and soon their eyes opened to Harry's service and they began
to grasp the message. Eventually Harry brought devoted followers together for Bible study and fellowship and served the
Lord in that forsaken place. Harry had become an extension
of Frankie's ministry behind the walls.

In spite of Frankie never dwelling on an inmate's past, Harry
had a message that he wanted to convey with all clarity – there
is no such thing as harmless indulgence in a joint. There is only

sad self-deception. That joint provides an escape that leads to lies, deceit, and manipulation, which destroy relationships and take control of the user – all while the user convinces himself he has it under control. For Harry, weekend use led to daily use and that led to complementing it with alcohol, which led to muddled thinking and circumstances that ended with a life sentence in prison. "Have a joint. Have a drink. Relax," they said.

Upon entering prison, mild tranquilizers were provided, but soon Harry needed more. Stronger drugs were readily available, so he moved through a variety of substances until he settled into narcotics – all while telling himself he had it under control. In hindsight, Harry could recognize that he turned to cheap liquor and a joint when he was not coping with reality, but he still thought he had it under control when the blood trickled from his arm as the needle went in and out. In prison, Harry saw many wasted lives that began with a seemingly harmless self-indulgence of one joint.

Harry's life is also an example of God never giving up on a person, no matter how low he has sunk. When Harry reached that point, he realized that the Christ that Frankie exemplified was his only answer and his only need. God led him to a blessed life of partnership with Frankie as he shared truth with other inmates.

Harry had become an assistant to Jason Browder, the previous house manager at the prison. While Frankie and Harry met for Bible discussions, Jason listened in. Harry's testimony impressed Jason so much that Harry was able to help shape Jason's Christian life. He took Harry's influence into his Sunday school class and then used it as director of Tracy's Camp, a mission to impact children for Christ. One more mission impacted by the ministry of Frankie San.

Harry was paroled after thirty-five years of incarceration – and transformation. Frankie took him shopping because he had never even seen a Walmart store before. "I feel like I've been in a coma and I've just come out," he related. Harry had been spiritually free for some time; now he was physically free too.

Jack

Jack sat outside the operations office at the old CCI, waiting to be processed and assigned a bed. He was a con man; Frankie was an easy target. In a short time, though, Frankie said to Jack, "You work for me at Christmas."

Jack said, "That was Frankie's style. He never asked if a guy wanted to do something; he told them, 'You will do whatever.' And the crazy thing was that everyone obeyed him. We're talking dudes with multiple life sentences who had killed in the world and in prison. We were all as meek as little lambs around Frankie."

Frankie discovered how well Jack could write vivid descriptions of his life experiences. He had lived among thieves and hopped trains as a hobo. He understood the homeless and alcoholics. Through Jack's writing, Frankie came to a better understanding of the world of hoodlums and hustling. Frankie could glean a wealth of lessons to help others from Jack's mistakes. The common thread that seemed to run through all and haunt so many of these inmates was inadequate or lack of parental guidance, especially a father figure.

When Jack was released from prison, he said his mentality was always that he knew he would be going back, so he'd party until they caught him. After years of incarceration, he found that he had lost his ability to make decisions – particularly the easy ones like what to eat, what to wear, when to go to bed, and when to get up. He admitted that he needed Frankie for support and guidance – and that made the difference.

Frankie declared, "Jack could con me all day, but he could

not con God. He is now beginning to see the light and I could not be happier."

Jack expressed his gratitude in these words: "Thank you for being more than a friend these past twenty-seven years. I can honestly say with no shame whatsoever that I love you, old man – from the bottom of my heart." As Jack grew in the Lord, their friendship grew also.

Jack related that Frankie's reputation and consistency empowered the message of the love of Christ more than words. Frankie's constancy forced the inmates to ponder how he could use a lollipop to bring a spiritual message. Jack said the hardest dudes there tell their young sons, "Man, that cat has been doing this for years because he's a real Christian." Stated as a fact. No comment necessary.

Jack's goal one year was to quit being critical of others. He said he would remind himself, "What would Frankie do or say?" He knew that with the wisdom and guidance of Frankie, he'd be able to correct his flaws. Maybe what he did not realize at the time was that what he saw in Frankie was really Christ.

Jack had quit writing when he was released from prison. Frankie thought of him every day and prayed for him every night. He did not know if Jack was alive or dead. Then, out of the blue, after two years of wondering, a letter from Jack arrived. He had been living out in the woods as a homeless person a few miles from Frankie. He became desperately sick with pancreas, liver, and stomach problems, so he got down on his knees and begged God to touch his life again. He recalled how rich his life had been at CCI when he acknowledged God as his only hope. He finally checked into the drug/alcohol program at Oliver Gospel Mission – the same mission that Frankie had visited during his seminary years.

At the mission, Jack attended Bible classes and studied the Word. He attended chapel twice a day and had classes three times a day. No visits. No passes. No unsupervised leaves unless it was medical or legal. Jack loved it. He believed that if he was left on his own, he'd mess up and die. He liked the Christ-centered life.

Jack was excited about his new life at the mission, and Frankie's spirit was revived and invigorated with a sense of joy as Jack continued to write about his growth. Frankie visited Jack and the life coaches he had at the mission. He pleaded with the coaches to have some flexibility with Jack because he had lived on the streets and in prison for so long, but he did not seem to make any headway with them, though Jack continued in their program. He just couldn't fit into society like the others.

One day Jack left the program. He told his coaches he couldn't continue, so Frankie suffered again. Frankie had experienced three months of invigorating new energy in serving Jack and encouraging him, but Jack left without an explanation. Frankie was down in the dumps again and couldn't pull himself out, although he concluded that even though Jack might never have been able to "make it" in normal society, he could influence his fellow street people in some positive way. So this was not necessarily a failure; it might be where he was meant to be.

Then, alcohol and street life claimed Jack one more time, but after a couple years and poor health, he dried out again. He acknowledged the difficulty of fitting in anywhere. Not at home. Not at church. Not at work. He found out that he did not even fit on the streets. He missed the camaraderie of jail and the sense of belonging. He felt shame and guilt, and dreams of prison haunted him, but he also remembered truths that Frankie taught him and turned to God for his strength. Jack did contact Frankie again and confessed to his wayward ways. The prodigal son had come home again.[74]

Harry and Jack were not the only ones who had been so

---

74   Adapted from *Cell 55*, Christmas 2009.

affected by Frankie's love and ministry that they too picked up their crosses and followed Christ. An inmate wrote that several other men had helped him. He said, "Now everything is real clear to me. It ain't all about us; it's about Jesus and His love for us. . . . Now I will help the next man that comes here, ya know?"

Ministry Multiplication

One particular event portrayed the extent of the ministry of Frankie San, and Charles penned an insightful perspective of the occasion – the graduation ceremony at Kirkland Correctional Institution. One of the men in the graduating class informed Charles that many in attendance were professors from Columbia International University (CIU) who were involved with the Seminary Initiative. Others were prominent figures from society – pastors, businessmen, and politicians. They all congregated in the library for this special graduation. Charles and his classmates chose to linger around the outside of this distinguished crowd. Charles wrote:

> To say that I was out of my element would be a major understatement. I was nervous and unable to comfortably communicate with anyone not wearing a tan uniform. . . . I could not understand the robed men sitting in front of me who were about to give speeches. How could I relate to them, or how could they understand me and the problems of my environment?
>
> One robe stood out to me during the CIU graduation ceremony. The well-known graduate and professor of ministry and love from the prestigious University of Hard Knocks: Frankie San donned

his doctoral colors of CCI. As he entered the room, I saw a symbol of true prison ministry and love. The robe he wore was a Santa Claus suit that he had worn for many years during his service to the *least of these.* I was able to identify with this honorable dignitary because he had been willing to step down to my level to comfort me.

Of all the men who were present and held master's and doctorate degrees, Frankie San was by far the greatest. During a moment when I felt so out of reach with the people around me, in walked this man who instantly calmed the storm. I am so grateful for the opportunity to work for Jesus under the direction of Frankie San.

I was happy that Frankie San was able to see the first group of prisoners graduate from a biblical university. They will be sent out like the disciples to minister and serve the needs of the twenty-four thousand men incarcerated in SCDC. They will go out and continue in a ministry that Frankie San began over forty years (at the time of this ceremony) ago, a ministry so much more than the use of one's tongue . . . it's all about love and action.

Later, Charles wrote to Frankie to tell him that he was creating a curriculum for training men in four areas of growth: (1) personal acknowledgment and accountability, (2) discipleship, (3) evangelism and ministry, and (4) basic study of the Word and New Testament survey. The CIU Prison Initiative sent Charles throughout the department as a missionary to other inmates. He connected with Jimmy, a former inmate from CCI who had written "Lonely Days, Lonely Knights." Jimmy had stated, "I may never get out of prison, but I have new life in Jesus Christ, and I want to help other guys with spiritual things. Though I may not see the outside of these prison walls, I see heaven in our future. . . . Freedom has been found within these cold, stone walls and razor-tipped fences, as my faith in Jesus Christ brings true and absolute freedom from sin and death. I am free in Jesus."

Charles commented that Jimmy had gone from death row and super maximum security to being a Character-Based Unit leader and mentor. Jimmy declared, "Charles and I both graduated from the Frankie San University of Higher Learning! Isn't God great?!"

Stephen also became one of Frankie's mission partners. He wrote to Frankie for the first time after Frankie had been turned away from his scheduled death row visit on February 17, 2011. Though he had never written before and had remained aloof during the visits, he told Frankie how the whole atmosphere would change when he came. He attributed that change to the "absolutely pure love and care for the prisoners" that was evident. Stephen was best able to express himself from a Christ-centered worldview and actively sought ways to serve the other death row inmates, but he also had connections outside the walls. He was an intelligent academic, an author, and a new believer who knew a criminology professor.

In fact, Stephen had an unusual outreach opportunity. One of his co-authors taught a graduate class; she asked him to talk to the class and answer questions via a cell phone connected to a microphone and speaker system. For almost two hours, he spoke with twenty-two students, even though he had to keep calling them back every fifteen minutes because it was a group phone. The students asked about the justice system, legal procedures, and conditions in the prison. Most importantly, they asked about faith-based programs, and he was able to tell about his personal journey with Christ. He even told them about Frankie and expressed that one person can make the difference in the life of an inmate. When Stephen had to end the call, the students gave him an ovation.

Though he didn't have the same resources as Frankie, Stephen was innovative enough to pull off a Christmas delivery from cell 218. Operation Frankie San Claus took a couple weeks because Stephen had limited dollars for the canteen. First, he made a complete list of everything he wanted to get each person. His goal was to give all of them something they needed, something they wanted, something special, some hygiene items, and some correspondence materials. Each individual would receive four or five items. Since Stephen lived with these men, he could personalize each gift.

After he created the list, he gave the canteen manager advance notice to ensure there was ample supply without depleting the canteen. The manager talked to Stephen about what he was doing, and the barrier that seemed to exist between inmate and staff disintegrated and disappeared. When canteen-day came, Stephen said he felt more like a kid at Christmas than one of Frankie's elves. The officers took two laundry bags and two boxes full of canteen items to Stephen's cell. The guys on the unit made comments about how much he had. Of course, they had no idea how much Stephen had spent or that the items were for them; the only thing Stephen requested for himself was a stamped envelope.

Stephen took the list and divided everything up – cell by cell. The officers were so amazed that they did all they could to help distribute the gifts. Stephen stood on the "rock" in the center and called out, "Attention on the rock!" He told them that the gifts were from "Frankie San Claus." Gifts of love.

Distribution was tricky because the officers also had to bring guys in from recreation, in and out of showers, and to and from attorney visits; then they had to serve lunch trays. The guys all gave their thanks to Frankie for remembering them and wished him a Merry Christmas. The whole distribution took about eight hours, and Stephen was exhausted, but much of that was from the day's emotional highs followed by the calm. By taking no credit for himself, Stephen then understood the exhilaration of the friendship, giving, and joy that energized Frankie all those years.

One of the most amazing aspects of this project was the impact that spread like wildfire even among the staff. Most of the officers came by Stephen's door and asked, "Do you mean everything you bought from the canteen was passed out to the inmates in the unit?" They seemed to recognize the immense levels of love, fellowship, and true kindness. Stephen only replied that it came from Someone and something far greater than him.[75]

Stephen told Frankie that he was blessed by his example. He learned how to go from reading God's Word and believing to walking the walk of faith. He could do more than talk the talk; he could live in the Spirit and walk the walk even in prison. (See Stephen's story "The Plumber" in Appendix B.)

Learning by Example

Joey first contacted Frankie when he wanted to transfer to Broad River Correctional Institution to assist the young inmates. He had been a white supremacist gang member from California who received Christ at the invitation of a black corrections officer. God does have a sense of humor. Joey attested to the fact that being locked down brings a person to the end of himself. Once self is removed, God can do a mighty work in that life.

The inmates watched Frankie – even more than they talked

---

75   Adapted from "Christmas from Cell 218," by Stephen, *Cell 55*, Christmas 2011.

with him. They saw his responses to ill treatment and harassment. They saw him smile and continue. They learned how to "walk" by watching him. Mark related his own act of kindness to Frankie: "I've never told you this, but this is what I do with the candy you bring: I always make sure the Ziploc bag is sealed tight; then I take all my candy and put it aside. I hold my candy for thirty days. Always. On the thirtieth day, I open my bag, take some out, and give it to my next-door neighbor. It doesn't matter who he is. I always break bread with whoever lives next door to me. Then I start eating my candy. I've done this every time you've come for many years." A small gesture, but in a facility where sharing is not common, it was remarkable. Truly, Frankie's work expanded and lived on beyond his physical presence within the walls.

Frankie's training of his helpers and coworkers was one of slow, methodical example. He didn't push or lecture. He led by living his life for Christ. By doing so, he impacted the lives of those he served in a way that they too wanted to experience the joy of serving.

Inmates continue to reminisce, relate, and reproduce aspects of Frankie's ministry and instruction. One time Charles and Harry befriended Patrick and included him in Bible study and their times of sharing at the Short Term Offender Program (STOP). They told their stories but also told about Frankie San and his love for the inmates. When Harry asked if Patrick could join them as an elf to distribute Christmas gifts, Frankie said, "The little redheaded guy? Yeah, sure." Patrick was thrilled that he would actually have the opportunity to meet the famous Frankie San.

What a blast it was! Patrick was finally getting to know the little Japanese giant who had been God's instrument to change so many hardened criminals. He found Frankie's love contagious and saw why joy had spread throughout the hearts of society's worst of the worst. He helped distribute apples and bananas, Texas cinnamon buns, and candy that day.

When they finished, Santa and his elves went back to the chapel where Frankie told them to sit on chairs in a circle – each with a paper grocery sack in front of him. They played games and got prizes. They laughed and even screamed. What an abundance! Whole bags of chocolate bars and sodas, more fruit, and many other goodies. After all the laughs and fun, he told them to choose their favorite thing from their sacks; then he told them to give it to the person they liked the least. Now, that was a new thought, but in this way, Frankie taught them about giving and denying oneself. He taught them about losing their lives to find their lives. He showed them by his own example, but then helped them realize that they could imitate the same selfless giving.

One day Patrick wrote Frankie a thank-you letter and told him a little about his own life and the two daughters he had to leave behind. After reading the letter, Frankie called him to the chapel and asked for the address of the two girls so he could do something nice for them. Patrick learned later from his mother that Frankie had come bearing gifts. Four dolls – a collector's doll in a giant box for each girl and a Cabbage Patch doll for each. The whole family experienced the love of Christ through that act of kindness from Frankie.

As Frankie reached and trained his "brothers" and "sons," they in turn continued the mission – to reach others with the love of the Lord. *A new commandment I give to you, that you love one another, even as I have loved you, that you also love one another. By this all men will know that you are My disciples, if you have love for one another* (John 13:34-35).

Chapter 20

Frankie's Wisdom

On Friday, June 1, 2007, Senator Ronnie Cromer presented Frankie with the Order of the Silver Crescent award for a lifetime of volunteer service. Bishop Donges presented him with a pectoral cross, hand-carved by Pastor Dermon Sox from the wood of a cherry tree, which had grown on the seminary campus.[76] Governor Mark Sanford sent this note:

> "You capture the essence of a gentleman who considers it a privilege to serve others, and I am reminded of Micah 6:8. *He has told you, O man, what is good; and what does the* LORD *require of you but to do justice, to love kindness, and to walk humbly with your God?*"[77]

To this point, David R. Barnhart said:

> At times that gentle man of God, with meek and loving spirit, has eyes filled with tears. There are

---

76   "Frankie San Honored by the Governor's Office and the SC Synod," *South Carolina Lutheran*, July-August 2007, p. 3.

77   Excerpt from *Cell 55*, 2007.

times when his step slows and when he wonders
how he can continue day after day; times when
his heart nearly breaks over the human frustration of so rich a treasure in so frail a vessel. But
lonely voices call and Frankie is off again to share
– to give. But Frankie has never called attention to
the vessel, but only to the "treasure." Whether it
is in the prison cell or in congregations across the
land, Frankie draws attention only to Jesus and the
power that He gives to live.[78]

Throughout four decades of writing in *Cell 55*, Frankie San shared
much wisdom for his readers. Here are some of his thoughts:

"As I reached out to these people, I sensed that
Jesus was there among us. There is no other way I
can explain it. God really loved me and I was able
to touch these unlovable men. No one has seen
the Lord, but He was living inside me. How much
more can I tell you? I could not love them unless
God loved me. It was not me. God loved these men
through me."

Another time he said:

Yes, I have gone through my share of struggles in
this life, and I have had to sacrifice many things;
yet these guys in prison, with such desperation
and crushed wills, are still proclaiming the good
news of Jesus Christ amidst all their pain. This is
my message after forty years – God works His plan
through our struggles, no matter what they may be,

---

78   Excerpt from *Cell 55*, Summer 2011.

and He never allows us more than we can handle in this life. He helps us to make it when all is seemingly lost, destroyed, or forgotten. God gave us the greatest gift when He sent His Son into this world, because the babe, the Christ, would bring us hope.

After September 11, 2001, Frankie's sister wrote to express how worried she was for him – particularly since he received so much mail. She was also concerned for the way the world was changing. Frankie responded that she was right. He said:

The family is breaking down and God is being abandoned; the outcome is we don't have anything left to cling to. . . . The Lord never said this life would be easy, without struggle, without suffering. But in the struggles and in the suffering, whether at home or abroad, in war or in peace, God is there abiding in the hearts of His people. And when we reach down to help somebody else and share what God has done for us, the Holy Spirit reveals Himself and that brings the richest life. . . . Jesus Christ gave me strength to leave everything, to come follow God, and to serve the most forgotten men behind the bars. They in turn taught me all about my life and helped me discover my value as a Christian.[79]

For God, who said, "Light shall shine out of darkness," is the One who has shone in our hearts to give the Light of the knowledge of the glory of God in the face of Christ. We are afflicted in every way, but not crushed; perplexed, but not despairing; persecuted, but not forsaken; struck down, but not destroyed;

---

79 Excerpt from *Cell 55*, Christmas 2001.

always carrying about in the body the dying of Jesus, so that the life of Jesus also may be manifested in our body. (2 Corinthians 4:6, 8-10)

As Frankie contemplated the problem of overcrowding in the prisons, he recognized that prisoners seemed to be younger and younger with each passing decade. The numbers went up and the ages went down. He did not believe that newer, bigger prisons and stiffer penalties were the answer to control crime in society. He saw the need for strong families with fathers who serve God. He said, "I have few solutions to crime except the Word of God; to me, God is the only solution."

"On Splitting Rocks" by Dwayne Westermann

Frankie did not spend a lot of time writing about himself; he used his time to reach out and touch others for the Lord. He wanted them to experience the love of God. So we look to the writings of those who knew him to grasp a portion of his wisdom. Dwayne was one such writer that Frankie cared about. He wrote a vivid picture of strength and perseverance of Frankie San entitled "On Splitting Rocks."

There is a place not far from here in the Blue Ridge Mountains where the Appalachian Trail winds its way deep into a river-cut gorge. In the bottom of this gorge stands a tree, a pine tree. That would not be worthy of note in itself, for there are thousands of others just like it, except that this particular pine tree grows out of a crack in an enormous rock, a limestone boulder, that weighs many tons.

What apparently happened was that a seed fell into a very small crack in the boulder years ago and somehow managed to sink its roots down into the life-giving earth underneath the rock and began to grow. As it grew taller, it grew also in diameter and, fragile as it was, actually pushed tons of rock apart, until today, the tree is probably a foot in diameter. The enormous pressure of the rock continues to push on the tree, and the tree continues its struggle to split the rock. And even though no movement is apparent, one can sense the terrific tension that exists between the two.

This particular pine tree always makes me feel that some words of congratulation and encouragement are in order. It's a fantastic achievement when you stop to think about it. The tree continues to grow larger year after year, even though it must do so in spite of the tension from the great pressure in the jaws of the rock. And amazingly, the rock continues to be split wider and wider, not by the kind of explosive force that we usually associate with such a thing, but by the slow, steady, unrelenting perseverance of that growing tree. It is almost as if that tree hoped for something that was altogether impossible, to grow under such circumstances, and yet, it continued to achieve it. It is a tension, a tension of hoping for the impossible, of expecting what cannot be rightly or reasonably expected.

That same tension exists for a friend of ours. Many of us have met and have come to love Frankie San, the Japanese Santa Claus, the Lutheran chaplain at the state penitentiary in Columbia, South Carolina. To walk the poorly lighted corridors of that prison with Frankie is an experience. He'll point and tell you, "Here's where I was trapped when the first riot broke out," and "I take my nap in this cellblock; the bunk belongs to a murderer." "This is where one of my students was stabbed to death; why do they do such things?" he'd ask.

And there are a dozen other places in the bowels of that prison where Frankie recalls the tensest experiences that would have sent most people pleading to get out. And yet, he stays. To look into the faces of the inmates removes all doubt that there is terrible tension that exists for Frankie in his work there. And yet, he stays. Why?

Because he hopes for the impossible and expects that which he has no business expecting. He is like a very small tree struggling to grow through a very large rock. In his own words, he describes that terrible tension: "What pain and struggle. The animals in zoos are treated more kindly. Trying to understand the agonies of these men, I tried to become like them. I tried every possible way to live like them: eating the same meals, taking naps with murderers, and talking with them late at night. I thought I could understand their struggle, but after a few years, I realize my understanding may never be complete. As long as I live, I will try. There can be no real Christian life without struggling."

To know Frankie and what he has accomplished is to know that while the pressure and tension of that rock is always there, he continues to grow through it by slow, steady, unrelenting perseverance.

Christians are people who expect what they have no business expecting, and hope for things impossible. . . . When we look at this small tree splitting the great rock, when we see this frail man sleeping in a murderer's bed, we must step back and recognize that God does not deal with His world on the basis of reasonable expectations and right hopes. . . . God roots us into life-giving earth and loves us into trying to grow against the suffocation of our own self-centeredness that presses against us, that resists our growing.

That is how Dwayne saw Frankie – nothing but a seed that landed in a small crack of a very large rock. But knowing how God strengthens us and helps us grow through the tensions and struggles, Frankie persevered and taught his brothers to do likewise.

Final Thoughts

As Frankie prepared bags of candy, his mind kept asking God, "Lord, how long shall I do this? How long? I'm just getting old. How many more years? I've worked all during my retirement, but where is the ending?" He was seventy-eight at that time – and tired.

As Frankie worked, he started becoming forgetful, so he made an appointment with the doctor and had tests run. When the doctor told him he had Alzheimer's disease, he said, "Okay. That's what it is." Then he realized that God had answered his question. His days were numbered. Rather than hide the fact, he started telling everyone that he might not remember their names. He took his medication but lost all desire to do anything. He didn't even eat.

One day he had his coffee and went out to get the mail. One letter written by an inmate who was back in prison caught his attention. The guy was asking for help. Right then it dawned on Frankie – he was still needed. That same afternoon he wrote a long letter to this inmate; Frankie was revived by the great needs of the men.

He said, "I had almost nothing when I came to this country. Now fifty years later, I have nothing but Jesus Christ. I have lived alone; I have nobody, no family. But all these lowly people came along, and they loved me as I loved Jesus. What more can I ask for in my lifetime? These beggars, thieves, and rapists say, 'We love you, Frankie.' One word: we are looking for love. God is love. We are all searching for love."

Frankie had a message for his friends – even with his struggles, his life was not finished. God could still use him whatever his condition. He would continue to visit the prison; he would write letters; he would fight the good fight and finish his race.[80]

---

80   Adapted from *Cell 55*, Christmas 2007.

With his failing health, Frankie's work with his ministries slowed up, but that often left him "in the pits." He had discovered that prisoners struggle to go from prison to society and its freedom. Soldiers struggle to go from war to home and normalcy. He struggled too. He struggled to go from full-time institutionalized ministry to retirement and idleness. He felt like a war veteran. The pain and suffering from the years were difficult, but they made his life rich in Jesus Christ. He knew that *the sufferings of this present time are not worthy to be compared with the glory that is to be revealed in us* (Romans 8:18). He found renewed purpose in these words:

> As long as we have the light of day,
> we must work –
> not to conquer, acquire,
> accumulate, and retire,
> but to make visible the invisible Christ
> and to touch men and women,
> boys and girls, with His love.[81]

---

81   Author unknown.

Appendix A

Biographical Sketch of Kyuzo Miyaishi (Frankie San)

September 1929: Birth of Kyuzo Miyaishi in Tokyo, Japan

May 1944: Joined Imperial Japanese Navy during World War II

July 1961: Arrival in America

September 1961: Enrolled in Columbia Bible College

January 1962: Transferred to Lutheran Theological Southern Seminary, Columbia, SC

June 1965-May 1966: Internship at the Lutheran Children's Home, Salem, VA; attended Roanoke College, Salem, VA

May 1966: Graduated from Lutheran Theological Southern Seminary with a master's in Religious Education

May 1966-1975: Adult Education teacher at Central Correctional Institution's Education Department

1967-1975: Attended University of South Carolina

May 1973: Ordained by South Carolina Synod (Tentmaking Ministry)

May 1975: Transferred to library staff

1985: Employee of the Year Award for South Carolina Department of Corrections

May 1991: Completed twenty-five years of prison work

1994: CCI closed

1994-1998: Moved to Kirkland infirmary to work with HIV/ AIDS patients

1998-2001: Retirement; continued part-time work

2001: Retirement due to budget cuts; continued working as a volunteer

June 2007: Received Order of the Silver Crescent award for a lifetime of volunteer service

Appendix B

Frankie's Collections

Prisoner Poems

Frankie did not collect coins, stamps, or antiques like other people. When he began his ministry, he knew his rewards could not be measured in money or material things, but he did collect words and art. He kept and cherished the many things that the men in prison had written or made for him: letters, stories, poems, cards, paintings, and crafts. They spoke of his love, his mission, his life, and his influence on their lives. For this reason, some have been included in the previous chapters and more are included here.

From an essay entitled "Two Different Worlds":

> There are prisons made by man
>   of iron bars and stone.
> There are prisons of the mind,
>   and each man makes his own.
>   – Bob

Long before a judge sentenced me to a penitentiary cell, I built for myself a prison much stronger than brick, mortar, and steel. I was trapped in the world of my own choosing, and try as I might, I could not find my way into that other world that was all around me, where God ruled and where men obeyed and found satisfaction and happiness, even joy, in being obedient.

I have been fortunate. Despite all my efforts to keep Him out, God came into my world. He sent a man with His unselfish love to guide me out of the prison world I had constructed and into life and freedom.

That man was Frankie San, and Bob's changed life and love of God is the living proof that the ministry/service/love of Frankie has everlasting results in the prison world.[82]

The Choices We Make

There are choices to make –
To give or to take –
   As daily we live or die.
And the one brings life, while
The other brings strife
   Or a prison wall built high.
As strange as it seems, if
We plan and we scheme
   To take, we can only lose;

---

82   Adapted from an excerpt from "Two Different Worlds," by Bob, *Cell 55*, March 1967.

And we cause less pain
To ourselves, and gain,
    If it's giving that we choose.
It doesn't seem just
Somehow that we must
    Give away the things we need.
But within our heart
It is hard to part
    The necessities from greed.
Yet there is a way
That day by day
    We can know which choice to make.
We can simply ask
At each fork in the path,
    "Which way would He have me take?"
And we mustn't look back
On our chosen track,
    Or ask what others may do.
For it's plain to see
What is right for me
    May not be the choice for you.
But there's one great plan
For the race of man,
    And God has a role for us all,
And we'll meet some day
As we go our way,
    If we've chosen to follow His call.[83]
    – Bob

---

83   "The Choices We Make," by Bob, *Cell 55*, March 1967.

The Tax

Now in those days a decree went out from Caesar
Augustus, that a census be taken of all the
inhabited earth. – Luke 2:1

'Twas on the road to Bethlehem
    A dusty, weary band
Of humble travelers made their way,
    For Caesar did command.

They walked the miles from Naz'reth,
    The narrow, wind-swept track.
But Caesars issue their decrees;
    The subjects bring the tax.

One man a simple carpenter,
    His wife was great with child,
And though the road was rocky, steep,
    Perhaps she wore a smile.

Because I think she knew that day
    Time enough would be to grieve,
But on the road to Bethlehem
    'Twas the first Christmas Eve.

We now know all that happened
    When they reached the town.
How at the inn where they would rest
    A room could not be found.

She gave birth in the stables.
    Her bed, the hoof-trod ground.
But then a strange and wondrous thing,
    The Magi gathered round.

Such an enchanted story!
    The star, and its great light,
And how it shown on flocks of sheep
    And gave the shepherds fright.

They told how hosts of angels sang
    As they watched with the herds.
And then we see quiet Mary,
    But she speaks not a word.

On that first Christmas day she sat
    And pondered in her heart.
As if in the events that passed
    She wished a smaller part.

Oh, what did Mary think about?
    I think her thoughts may well have been
The tax that must be paid.[84]
    – Bob

The Washmachine Kid

This is the story both silly and bold
    The likes of which have never been told.
It's about a guy I'm sure you all know,
    And home was the place he wanted to go.

Now this guy was in prison and had been for a while.
    He'd been there so long, even his face went out of style.
To himself he said, "Custody 'A' I must make;
    Why, they shouldn't mind giving me this one little break."

---

84   "The Tax," by Bob, *Cell 55*, December 1967.

He put on his best shirt and combed up his hair,
  And in front of the board he stepped with great flair.
The board turned him down, the reason was not clear;
  Then his only thought was, "I've got to get out of here."

Then it came to him in a dream, bush parole he would make,
  Bush parole being prison slang, meaning a prison break.
If they won't let me go, then I'll go on my own.
  The plans I will make and it shouldn't take long.

Now the fences are too high and the walls are too steep,
  So out the front gate, I guess I must creep.
What I'll do is arrange for the use of a truck,
  And my mother's washmachine, it will be sent to pick up.

I studied it long and I studied it hard.
  Why, I could have them deliver to my mother's backyard.
In the washmachine, I knew I could hide,
  And there I would wait till they shipped it outside.

The washmachine arrived without much decision;
  I took out the motor and also the transmission.
If I bent and I curled, I could just fit inside;
  Who would ever think of such a place to hide.

I worked for maintenance, in this I took pride;
  At no other job could I have taken this ride.
I climbed in and sat next morning at eight,
  And then I began my final little wait.

Sure enough, in a minute or two
  Here came the truck with the loading crew.
They loaded me up and away I did ride;
  You better believe it was cramped inside.

We rode and we rode for ten minutes or more,
And then I heard the driver knock on Mom's back door.
He said, "Here's your machine fixed up like brand new."
I wanted to giggle but what could I do?

I stayed gone two days and what fun I did have,
But when they caught me, it made me so sad.
The Warden blew his top, he jumped up and down;
"Son, you had it made," he said with a frown.

Since that day long ago, that I did what I did,
I've always been called the washmachine kid.
My story is odd but I swear it's the truth;
See here, I'm living proof.
Could I have "A" custody, Warden?[85]
    – #62552

(Untitled)

Oh, to be free to follow the sun,
To feel the wind and rain;
To turn back the clock in all I have done;
And live life over again.

To walk through life, my head held high,
With never a doubt of my way;
Instead of living a fruitless lie,
The way I am living today.[86]
    – Pat

---

85   "The Washmachine Kid," by #62552, *Cell 55*, January 1977.
86   From *Work of Faith, Labor of Love, Steadfastness of Hope*, by Frankie San.

(Untitled)

I sit here and wonder as days plod by,
    Of mountains and meadows and sun in the sky.
Of flowers that bloom and breezes that sigh;
    And I wonder, though knowing, who am I?

I am the convict forever alone
    Whose heart is as dead and as cold as a stone.
Whose soul was damned before it was born,
    And as formless as mist on a cold, foggy morn.

I think of a forest so green in the rain,
    And I know that I'll never walk there again,
And knowing I know life's not worth the pain,
    For my life is hopeless; it shows in my name.

My name is a number, first, middle, and last,
    Which has no future, only a past;
My future is dead, my lot has been cast,
    Of freedom, my eyes have seen their last.

I can still see the grass growing green in the dell,
    A house painted white and a roof covered well,
And a brook that's as clear as the note of a bell,
    But I can't see myself and why I can't tell.

Is the pain of this prison blinding my eye?
    I see only the clouds, not the birds in the sky.
I seek not to live but only to die,
    For what worth is a convict such as I?

Then comes a man, yellow of skin,
    In the sea of life he's a fisher of men.
He says life's not over but only begin,
    And I push him away as I have with all men.

But no matter how hard I push him away,
    He comes back again, in a week or a day,
For he won't be put off in what he must say:
    That he'll pick me up when I fall by the way.

What is it about him that quickens my heart,
    That makes me believe I could have a new start?
I really can't tell, he's a man set apart,
    And I hear his word in the depth of my heart.

Now I sit and I wonder as days plod by
    Of a small yellow man with love in his eye,
Who asks me to live, who don't want me to die,
    Who answers my question: who am I?

You are the convict who is never alone,
    Whose heart is much valued by God on His throne,
Who is shaped in the form that God called His own,
    Whose soul was much blessed on the day it was born.[87]
    – Pat

Santa San Frankie

He rode into town one crisp December night,
    Dressed in a suit of red, shining with inner light.
Where he came from, no one could really say.
    He just appeared at the prison gates on that snowy
    winter's day.

He spoke with an accent, though his words were clearly heard.
    "Ho, Ho, Ho," said Santa San Frankie in a voice with
    love and care.
"It's Santa San Frankie," cried a prisoner from his lonely cell.
    Then another shouted, "I thought I heard Christmas bells."

---

87   Excerpt from *Work of Faith, Labor of Love, Steadfastness of Hope*, by Frankie San.

"Go back to sleep you two," exclaimed a prison guard nearby.
"There's no such thing as Santa San Frankie. Next thing
you'll tell me he can fly."
He laughed and chuckled at his joke,
Then leaned back in his chair to light a smoke.

As I turned away, my excitement growing dim,
I heard a voice and jingling bells faintly once again.
"Ho, Ho, Ho! Merry Christmas," arose the wonderful loving
sound.
And my heart beat faster at the hope which I had found.

It's Santa San Frankie ringing bells and spreading cheer,
Bringing hope, love, and warmth throughout the
Christmas year.
He sings a song then clicks his heel, as he visits every cell,
Passing out his gifts of love where misery is said to dwell.

The tiers of cells came to life as the hopeless struggled to see
This little Japanese Santa who loved them all in spite of
their degree.
"Now remember," he smiled as he turned to go upon his way,
"Jesus Christ loves you all and He was born on Christmas
Day."

I stood there watching as he disappeared without a trace,
And felt tears of happiness spill down upon my face.
Many were thankful for the gifts given them that day,
For Santa San Frankie brought peace and joy to stay.

Later, as I sat in silence, it was then I did believe,
A smile creased my face at the true gift I had received.
– For Frankie San. With much love, Drew. 1997[88]

---

88   *Cell 55*, Christmas 2006.

"The Plumber" by Steve

The day was busier than most, and standing at my door again was the plumber. This was not the first, second, or third time he had been called out. The equipment, so old and run-down, was in need of repair, and parts were extremely difficult to come by; gaskets were in short supply and the work area was nearly impossible to access. Consistent to his usual demeanor, the plumber stood before me explaining his intentions, conveying the many frustrations that accompanied his service calls to such a place.

"It's so hard to get back here sometimes," he said. "Getting all the tools I need to this area is never easy; and there's always a chance of getting stuck, especially if I need parts I don't have."

The plumber is a good man; he never points a finger at us. But, in a childish fashion, he often vents his frustrations to elevate our appreciation for his services. Notwithstanding this, any ill-spoken word contributes to the already negative atmosphere of this place. It's what it is. If you want to add life to a fire, you give it air. That's the easiest way to explain life here on death row.

As the plumber ended his grumbling, the area suddenly exploded with activity. The plumber stood in amazement as it unfolded; he'd never seen such a spectacle. His eyes transfixed and mouth agape, he made only one movement to step slightly closer to my cell door to keep away from the busy traffic.

Officers moved across the tiers, reaching into large cardboard boxes, distributing items to each cell. There was laughter and excitement on the block, suddenly charged with energy and emotion where moments before there had been lifelessness and despair. As I watched the plumber's face, I witnessed the very moment his disbelief became manifest.

"What the . . . ?" he said, as he observed the little Japanese man whose diminutive frame encased in red, white, and blue resembled a living emblem of national patriotism. I laughed. I had the same reaction the first time I saw Frankie San.

Not more than 125 pounds soaking wet, this small figure walked from cell to cell, shaking hands with the condemned. As best they could, the inmates reached through the bars and attempted to hug Frankie San in return. At each stop, the plumber could see the men offering their affections, words of love and friendship, and calling out from every corner of the block. There was laughter and conversation in every direction.

I watched the plumber turn his gaze from Frankie San toward an area downstairs. He'd seen another figure moving around the unit too – Frankie San's assistant joined in the gala celebration of life now occurring.

Before the plumber could speak, I said, "Don't worry, that's Frankie's sidekick. They're a team that knows no match." Instead of giving explanation to it all, I chose instead to wait and let the plumber absorb everything going on.

Frankie San and his assistant are an event best experienced. For more years than I have been alive, Frankie San has entered, walked in, lived in, and dealt with the hollows of some of the worst places in existence, among the inmates of death row, super max, and institutions all over South Carolina. He knows no fear in any prison setting. He shakes hands and hugs men whom most fear, those seen as the worst of the worst.

The plumber continued experiencing new thoughts and emotions. He stood perfectly silent as Frankie San stepped in between us to reach out and take my hand.

"We've missed you so much," I said as I shook Frankie's hand and placed my other upon his shoulder.

Frankie San smiled from ear to ear. "We so grad to see awe of you too. We love you!" he said. The plumber's eyes went back and forth between Frankie San and me as if he were watching a high-speed tennis match.

"Frankie San," I said, pulling him close, "we love you; we're so incredibly lucky to have you."

As Frankie San let go of my hand to move on to the next door, he instantly grabbed the plumber's hand and shook it. He smiled and looked into the plumber's eyes. "Harrow, how are you?" Frankie said.

Suddenly the plumber was looking at me. He needed some answers. Frankie San continued going cell to cell, shaking hands, talking briefly, and passing out bags of candy, bananas, honey buns, and other simple pastries. As we spoke, the plumber's gaze never left Frankie San for long.

"What church are they with?" he asked.

"They're with the church of God, the church of love, the church of goodness," I said. With that, the plumber's face revealed a look of slight disbelief, such as when one encounters for the first time selflessness, decency, and love which expects nothing in return.

In the following moments, I told the plumber Frankie's story – that he'd been a sailor in the Imperial Navy at fourteen. After the war, Frankie's beliefs and world had been torn apart and put in disarray. Frankie had struggled for years to recuperate and help his family. At twenty-seven, as a university student, Frankie had unsuccessfully attempted suicide and then found God.

Frankie San became a Christian. At thirty-two, he quit his job and came to America where he encountered many more obstacles: language barriers, various failures, and much doubt.

In seminary, Frankie San worked at hamburger joints and spoke to many people about life in the United States. He learned to communicate with people and learned of many troubles in the world. One day, a prison bus appeared – the sign that gave Frankie San's life meaning and understanding.

"I must visit the prison," he said. For years, Frankie San has worked, loved, and lived in the prison setting. Frankie's message is simple and constant: "Christ loves you; Christ forgives you. And that means Frankie San loves you too."

"I've worked in prisons in South Carolina and New York, and I've seen a lot of things in my life," the plumber said, "but I've never seen anything like this. I've been on death row countless times, and I've never seen such energy, life, spirit, joy, and peace." The plumber pointed around the block. "Look, every inmate is at his cell door smiling, laughing, and actually looking happy."

Suddenly, the plumber's face took on a solemn appearance. "There are people who wouldn't like seeing this. I bet there are people who wouldn't want death row inmates to receive such treatment."

"That's probably true," I said, "but that would also reveal much about them. No Christian or God-loving person would desire to keep beating down someone condemned to death. Jesus spoke to those in prison. He received hookers, vagrants, thieves, and every nature of person. If you ask me, it's the person like Frankie San who sees the good in everyone that I'd rather have walking the streets. A man who can promote hope, joy, and peace in here is a man that can show the world how to live out there."

The plumber, now apparently comfortable, looked me in the eye. "Steve, in an ideal world, you would be right. In the real world, an inmate on death row isn't received well by the public. It's what it is."

"What about you?" I asked. "How do you feel about it?"

"This is the most amazing thing I've ever seen," he said. "This place has been transformed from death into a place bristling with life. I'm going to tell my friends and family all about it."

"You know, the Bible addresses your concerns," I said. "To begin with, many of us here will be executed. Some will not.

Some may even die of natural causes before the state gets their chance. Regardless, we will all die at some point. No one lives forever." The plumber stared expectantly.

"As for those in the world who would refuse us the peace, joy, happiness, and love that Frankie San brings us, consider Galatians 5:22-23: *But the fruit of the Spirit is love, joy, peace, patience, kindness, goodness, faithfulness, gentleness, self-control; against such things there is no law.* That's what Frankie San is about."

The plumber's face was somber and he breathed heavily. "Even still, people in society don't want to see death row inmates given such comforts."

As an inmate on death row, I'd toiled with the same issue, but Frankie San's example had given me understanding. I shared it with the plumber. "Even if society were to forgive me, it's not as if I would suddenly walk free. That's a misunderstanding. God says, *Hate evil, love good, and establish justice in the gate!* (Amos 5:15). In my life, I've done more good than bad, but knowing these good acts will not stop me from being executed, can you still forgive me? Why is it so hard for people to forgive? Forgiveness is the core of a loving God. . . . If you were to forgive me right now, I wouldn't leave death row just because you did."

The plumber looked at me with concern. "But don't you think you have to be judged?"

"I have been," I said. "I have already been judged by men and sentenced to death. If that happens, I'm okay with it. I can't stop what God has allowed. But it's the judgment from God I care about."

The plumber still seemed to wonder. "Steve, were you always like this? If you were, it only makes sense to say you probably wouldn't be here, right?"

"Show me the human being who is without sin," I said.

"Have I always been a good man? No, not nearly as good as I wish I'd been. Have I been an evil man? No, I've never wished to hurt anyone. Yet, I'm on death row. One incident in my life resulted in a horrible ending. Do you believe there's one person in the world who doesn't have at least one moment in life that they would change if they could? To say no would be lying. But how much do you continue to punish?"

I pointed to Frankie San. "That man, right there, doesn't see the need to keep punishing. He brings a little joy, a little peace, and a little love into this condemned man's heart."

The plumber noticed my seriousness. "Steve, you've always been nice to me. I've always found it hard to believe that you're in here, but I know you've heard people say it's easy to say you're a Christian in prison."

"I wasn't trying to convince you. You've experienced Frankie San's witness transforming this whole unit, right? As for me, *if anyone is in Christ, he is a new creature; the old things passed away; behold, new things have come* (2 Corinthians 5:17). Eternity is what matters. Frankie San gives us a few snacks, and a whole lot of peace, joy, and love. Frankie's witness points us to an eternity with God."

"Why do you think he does it?" the plumber asked. "Why try to bring it to death row?"

"It's who he is – and why not? Jesus said to preach to every creature. Who else would want to come back here? And, who needs it more? Jesus looked for the ones who needed it most. Frankie San is following that lead."

There was a long and heavy pause. The plumber's heart seemed to be racing and his eyes gave the appearance of deep, heart-felt thought. Then he spoke. "One last thing; you may be executed. No one else besides me and some other officers may witness Frankie's efforts. What then?"

"You forget God. It doesn't matter who sees it out there. If

Frankie brings us closer to God, he has done more with each visit than most people do in a lifetime. Frankie San is serving God, not man. As for me, I've got it made. Millions of people in society go to church trying to impress others with their godliness, only to spend the rest of the week forgetting about God. All I have to do is live my life with only God watching. It's a lot easier for me."

The plumber was finished and ready to leave, so we shook hands. "Steve, I will share this with my family and friends. They probably won't believe it, but I have to share this with someone."

I called out to him as he walked away. "If you do share this experience, Frankie San will have reached yet another!"[89]

---

89   "The Plumber," by Steve, *Cell 55*, Midwinter Report 2013.

Appendix C

Author's Last Words

The plumber may have thought that Frankie's ministry stayed in that one prison, but we know his words of love and forgiveness and his mission to reach the lost radiated from the South Carolina Central Correctional Institution outward. It spread to other institutions in the state and to California, Texas, youth group visitations, and associations with pastors and officials; his ministry and vision have multiplied. He proceeded from prison work in one prison to multiple prisons, hospice care, street work, and youth camps. His work will touch lives and minister in many directions through his students, his brothers.

Frankie's life exemplified his heart and his teachings. Above all else, Frankie loved God, and with that love, he loved the unlovable. He understood and lived out the truth of Galatians 2:20 – *I have been crucified with Christ; and it is no longer I who live, but Christ lives in me; and the life which I now live in the flesh I live by faith in the Son of God, who loved me and gave Himself up for me.*

Steve, and many other death row inmates, captured a central truth during their association with Frankie. Robert related that in a real sense, all of us are residents on death row, for truly *the wages of sin is death.* But Christ came and died in our place. He took our guilt, our sins, and our shame upon Himself. How great His love! You don't have to be in prison to be in bondage. If you have never believed in Christ to be your Savior and Lord, do it today.[90] Sometimes it's easier for death row inmates to recognize their need for God and His salvation than it is for those outside the walls. Those with terminal illnesses may accept their approaching end and reach out to God, but what about the healthy? What about those who live each day as though they are invincible? We are not promised tomorrow. Today may be our last. We all live on death row; many just don't realize it. They ignore the fact of numbered days, but *man is like a mere breath; his days are like a passing shadow* (Psalm 144:4).

---

90   Adapted from "Prison Ministry – Redeeming Lives in a Throw-Away Society," by David Barnhart, *The Vine and the Branches*, Vol. 13, Issue 1 (Winter 1998).

Other Similar Titles

Uncommon Character,
by Douglas Feavel

A captivating non-fiction anthology filled with heroic profiles, epic tales, and timeless parables. Each chapter introduces a memorable hero who challenged and changed the world in remarkable ways. You'll meet personalities who are historical and living, unknown and familiar, domestic and foreign. Prepare to encounter pilots, farmers, immigrants, missionaries, engineers, martyrs, businessmen, lawyers, pioneers, presidents, soldiers, writers, and scientists – their dynamic legacies are destined to become part of us and our heritage.

These are unique tales told with zest; these are unforgettable tales to long treasure. Enjoy the exciting portraits; then share them in family, church, workplace, outreach, and educational settings because that's where they began, and that's why they were written. The 26 stories will quickly find special places in heart and head, dwelling there to influence life's crucial choices.

Available where books are sold.

The Last of the Giants,
by Harry Rimmer

In its early years, Duluth was a gold mine for lumber barons. Men were employed as lumberjacks and worked like beasts, only to be tossed aside like used equipment when no longer needed. The grand forests were raped for their prime timber, the balance burned wastefully. The men were coarse and hard, but they had to be to survive. More than any other people that ever lived in our land, these old-time lumberjacks could truthfully say, "No man cared for my soul."

That is, until God sent three men to the great Northwoods of our country – Frank Higgins, John Sornberger, and Al Channer. These men blazed new trails of the Spirit and founded an empire for God. They reached a sector of humanity for which no spiritual work had ever been done before, storming the Northwoods with a consuming passion for Christ. And with that passion, they also brought a heart as big as all outdoors, a love for men that burned like a flame, and a desperate desire to see these men saved.

They Call Me Momma Katherine,
by Katherine Hines

Do you ever sell yourself short? That's what Katherine Hines did before she realized she was selling God short. After years of tragedies, Katherine learned that God could do more in her life than she ever imagined if she trusted Him and believed. She discovered that He wants to change lives through us and bless us in the process. Whoever we are, wherever we came from, God can use us to make a difference in someone's life.

Katherine's story begins with tragedies, but God touched her heart at a crusade and led her to Uganda as a missionary to the children. Leaving her prestigious job and home, she went to a land of mud huts and polluted water. In the midst of sickness and poverty, she loved and cared for the orphans of the war-torn country, as she faced witch doctors and Muslim agitators. Katherine shares her life story to help us know that we can all make a difference – if only we let God . . .

Available where books are sold.

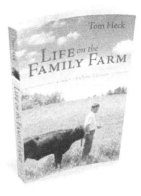

Life on the Family Farm,
by Tom Heck

"You are the most God-gifted writer I've ever had," Tom's college professor told him. However, Tom quit college; his love of farming drew him back to the farm. Thirty years later, Tom picked up the pen again, drawing readers into farming adventures with him. In these exciting and uplifting true stories, he shares his love of farming, family, and God. His unique writing style brings the reader right alongside him and his family as they work on their northern Wisconsin dairy farm.

Available where books are sold.

CPSIA information can be obtained
at www.ICGtesting.com
Printed in the USA
LVHW020524160720
660707LV00003B/74

9 781622 456475